Usborne

Visitors' Guide to

ANCIENT EGYPT

Based on the travels of Merymin

Compiled by Lesley Sims, Phil Clarke, Simon Tudhope & Louie Stowell

Illustrated by Peter Allen, Emma Dodd, Ian Jackson & John Woodcock

Designed by Marc Maynard, Karen Tomlins & Nayera Everall

Dear re

This book is based on my adventures in Ancient Egypt. You're in for a treat if you've never been before. I promise, you've never seen anything like it. It's almost like visiting another planet.

On my travels I took a lot of notes — and Lesley Sims, Phil Clarke, Simon Tudhope and Louie Stowell turned those dog-eared scribblings into this guide. (I wish I'd had one of these when I first went.)

Good luck!

Merymin*

*This, by the way, is my Egyptian name. I change my name as easily as I change my socks, and have a different one for every faraway place that I visit. But that's another story (or ten)...

Contents

The Basics

Into Upper Egypt

Thebes: temples and tombs

Nubia

Any other questions?

Internet links

This guide has all the information you'll need for your time tour of Ancient Egypt. But if you want to do some more (virtual) exploring, you can visit the Usborne Quicklinks Website, where you'll find links to fantastic websites. Just go to www.usborne.com/quicklinks and enter the keywords "guide to ancient egypt".

Before using the internet, please read the internet safety guidelines on the Usborne Quicklinks Website.

A note on dates

You'll see 'BC' after the dates in this book. This stands for 'Before Christ' - ancient dates are counted backwards from the year 0, when people thought Jesus Christ was born. So, what does that mean for your trip? Well, a journey back from the 21st Century to around 1000BC would mean you're going back 3,000 years into the past. Quite a trip.

Part one:
The basics

Thinking of a trip to Ancient Egypt? Be warned: if you don't know how to behave or what to expect, you could end up confused, embarrassed - or even dead.

But, there's no need to panic. I've put all the tips and tricks I learned on my Ancient Egyptian travels into this guide, so you should be fine. Let's begin with a few time-tourist basics, from what to take and when to go, to how to avoid getting ripped off in the first five minutes.

The first law of haggling: start low.

Mediterranean Sea
A trading ship bringing
imports of wine
and silver
The Nile
Delta
Sais
Tanis
Per Ramesses, capital of Ramesses II
Heliopolis
City of the
Sun God Re
A fort to
protect Egypt
against raiders
Giza The Pyramids
and the Sphinx
Memphis
Capital of the
Old Kingdom and
a thriving town
Western Desert
(sand as far as
the eye can see)
Sakkara Step pyramids
Lake Moeris
Middle Kingdom
pyramids
Red
Sea
To the copper
and turquoise
mines
N
Hermopolis
Eastern Desert
(wandering tribes
live here)
The fertile, green strips each side
of the Nile show the extent to
which the river floods each year.

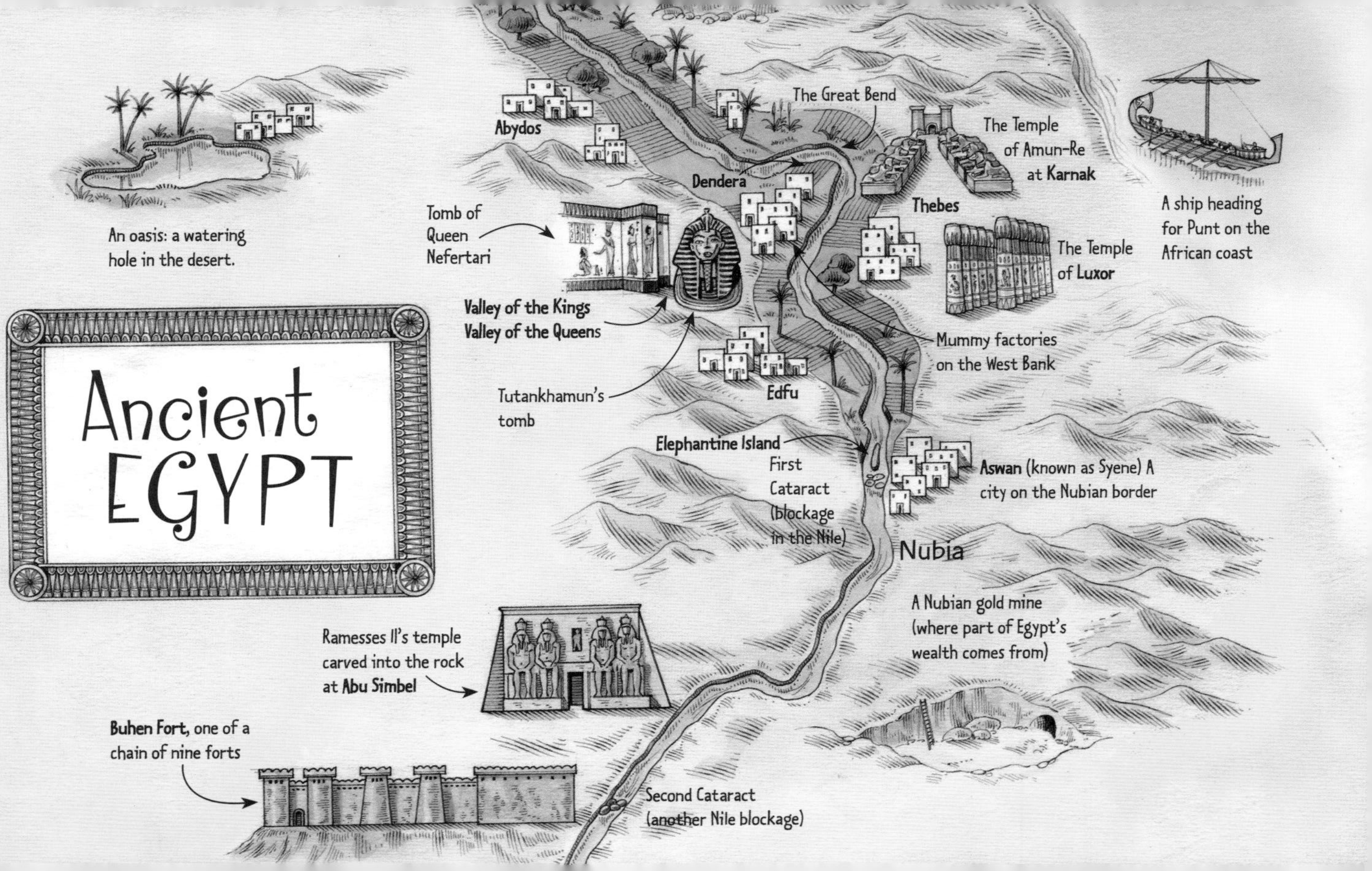
Ancient EGYPT
An oasis: a watering hole in the desert.
Abydos
Dendera
The Great Bend
The Temple of Amun-Re at Karnak
Thebes
A ship heading for Punt on the African coast
Tomb of Queen Nefertari
Valley of the Kings
Valley of the Queens
The Temple of Luxor
Mummy factories on the West Bank
Edfu
Tutankhamun's tomb
Elephantine Island
First Cataract (blockage in the Nile)
Aswan (known as Syene) A city on the Nubian border
Nubia
A Nubian gold mine (where part of Egypt's wealth comes from)
Ramesses II's temple carved into the rock at Abu Simbel
Buhen Fort, one of a chain of nine forts
Second Cataract (another Nile blockage)

Top tips for tourists

№ 1: Ouch!

Check your sandals for scorpions before putting them on, or you could get a nasty surprise.

Snakes are less of a problem because there aren't many around. But it only takes one snake to ruin your trip (and your chances of living past the next day) - so keep your eyes peeled.

What to expect

Ancient Egypt won't be an easy ride. There aren't any hotels or tour guides, and if you get into trouble, there's no embassy to help you. But, if you follow my advice, you'll find yourself comfy lodgings, and (fingers crossed) you'll either avoid trouble, or be able to use some of my tried and tested Egyptian-style methods for getting out of it.

Anyway, this beautiful country is worth any trouble. Under clear, blue skies you'll see astounding buildings, strange rituals, exotic markets, vast deserts and one of the world's greatest rivers - the Nile.

Packing and timing

Locals use leaf fans to keep mosquitoes at bay. Not 100% effective, but worth a try.

Winter's the best time to visit, avoiding the skin-baking, mozzie-swarming, summer heat. But don't pack your woolies - it'll still be hot. In fact, don't pack much at all. You'll be moving from place to place, so you don't want to be weighed down with bags.

One thing you should pack is pepper and other kitchen spices, and perhaps some silk if you have any at home. I'll tell you why in a minute. Oh, and take sunscreen.

Looking the part

Of course, Egyptians won't know what sunscreen is, so you'll have to be sly about putting it on. As for what to wear, you can buy clothes in most markets, so head to one early on. But do buy enough so you can change your clothes a few times a day. Egyptians are fanatical about cleanliness, so you'll get withering looks if you walk around with stains under your armpits and flies buzzing around you in delight.

How to pay for things

For small items, you can barter - that is, swap something you have for something you want. Bartering with the pepper (and maybe silk) you've brought will buy you a lot of nice stuff, as the Egyptians don't have either.

But people also use copper weights for money, so do sell some pepper to a merchant at a market to get yourself some of those, too.

The art of bribery

Some places aren't officially open, but many guards are willing to turn a blind eye in return for a suitable 'gesture of friendship'.

Here's how to do it:

Guard: Stop! The tomb's shut.

You: Oh. Ok. But maybe you're a little short of pepper right now?

Guard (shrugs): I'm always short of pepper. Come back in an hour... And bring the pepper.

(And you're in.)

Traders love to haggle - it's what makes their job fun, so don't be shy of striking a hard bargain.

If you look carefully, you can see that the king in this picture is wearing a red and white crown.

When to go

When people talk about Ancient Egypt, they could mean as far back in time as 5000BC (see page 6 for a reminder of what that means). But I don't recommend going back that far, unless you're really into farming. Back then, Egypt was just a cluster of villages and fields on the banks of the River Nile. Also, Egyptians from that time would never have seen a foreigner before, and they'd be more likely to welcome you with pointy weapons than open arms.

A far better time to visit is during the reign of Ramesses II, which is from about 1279 to 1213BC. Ramesses was a pharaoh - a king who's also a living god, a priest and basically the most amazing being on Earth.

This is based on the White Crown of Upper Egypt...

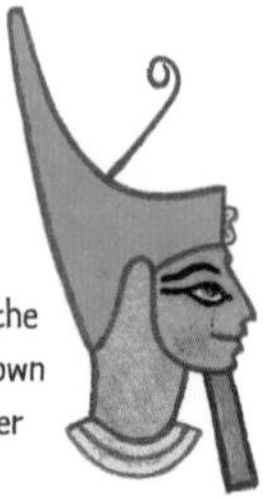

... and the Red Crown of Lower Egypt.

Egypt used to be split into Upper and Lower Egypt. These crowns date back to those days.

We are the greatest

During the reign of Ramesses II, Egyptian civilization is at its most mighty, dazzling and awe-inspiring. It's a place of giant pyramids and stunning palaces.

Though, if you ask an Ancient Egyptian, they've *always* been the greatest people on Earth. In fact, they're the *only* people: most foreigners aren't really people at all.

Lower is higher in Egypt

For a while, Egypt was split into two kingdoms - Upper and Lower Egypt - but it was squished into one big kingdom well before your visit.

People still think in terms of Upper and Lower Egypt though. Confusingly, Upper Egypt is below Lower Egypt on a map. It's based on the fact that the Nile flows from south to north - Egyptians take the Nile *very* seriously.

A slate carving of an Upper Egyptian king executing a prince from Lower Egypt.

A little more history

Egyptian history is split into periods, known as kingdoms. Ramesses was pharaoh during one of the most important: the New Kingdom.

This was already over a thousand years after the pyramids were built, but a thousand years before Cleopatra became Egypt's last pharaoh.

Don't worry about all that now. You can find out more on pages 120-125 if you're curious.

Pharaoh town

You'll probably come to rely on the Nile too. The River Nile runs the full length of Egypt, so boat trips up and down it are the best way to see the country, and most of the interesting stuff is clustered around it.

Even the capital city, Per Ramesses, is on the Nile. Ramesses II named the city after himself, which might sound smug. But if you were that powerful, I bet you'd be tempted to name a town or two after your great big important self.

Choose a boat with a canopy, so you'll be protected from the blazing sun.

> “Would that I were in the country always...”
>
> From a manuscript written by a proud local

How to get to Ancient Egypt

Once you've arrived in the right year, you'll probably need more detailed directions.

Since Egypt is surrounded by desert on three sides, it's easiest to arrive by boat across the Mediterranean Sea. But if you call it that, Egyptians will stare at you blankly - they call it the Great Green, and you should take their lead.

After all, the Ancient Egyptians always know best about absolutely everything (according to the Ancient Egyptians).

It'll be a relief to step on shore after so long at sea.

Egyptian etiquette

Egyptians are a welcoming people but they have a particular way of doing things. There are a number of books doing the rounds that give advice on how to behave in company.

It's well worth picking up a second-hand copy if you want to fine-tune your Egyptian manners.

You, too, can become human

As you aren't an Ancient Egyptian, the locals will probably look down on you. As far as they're concerned, foreigners are savages. Actually, they're worse than savages - they're not even human beings.

But don't despair. Egyptians will treat you like a proper, civilized person if you act just like them. I'll be giving you tips about how to do this all through the book. But the main trick seems to be washing a lot.

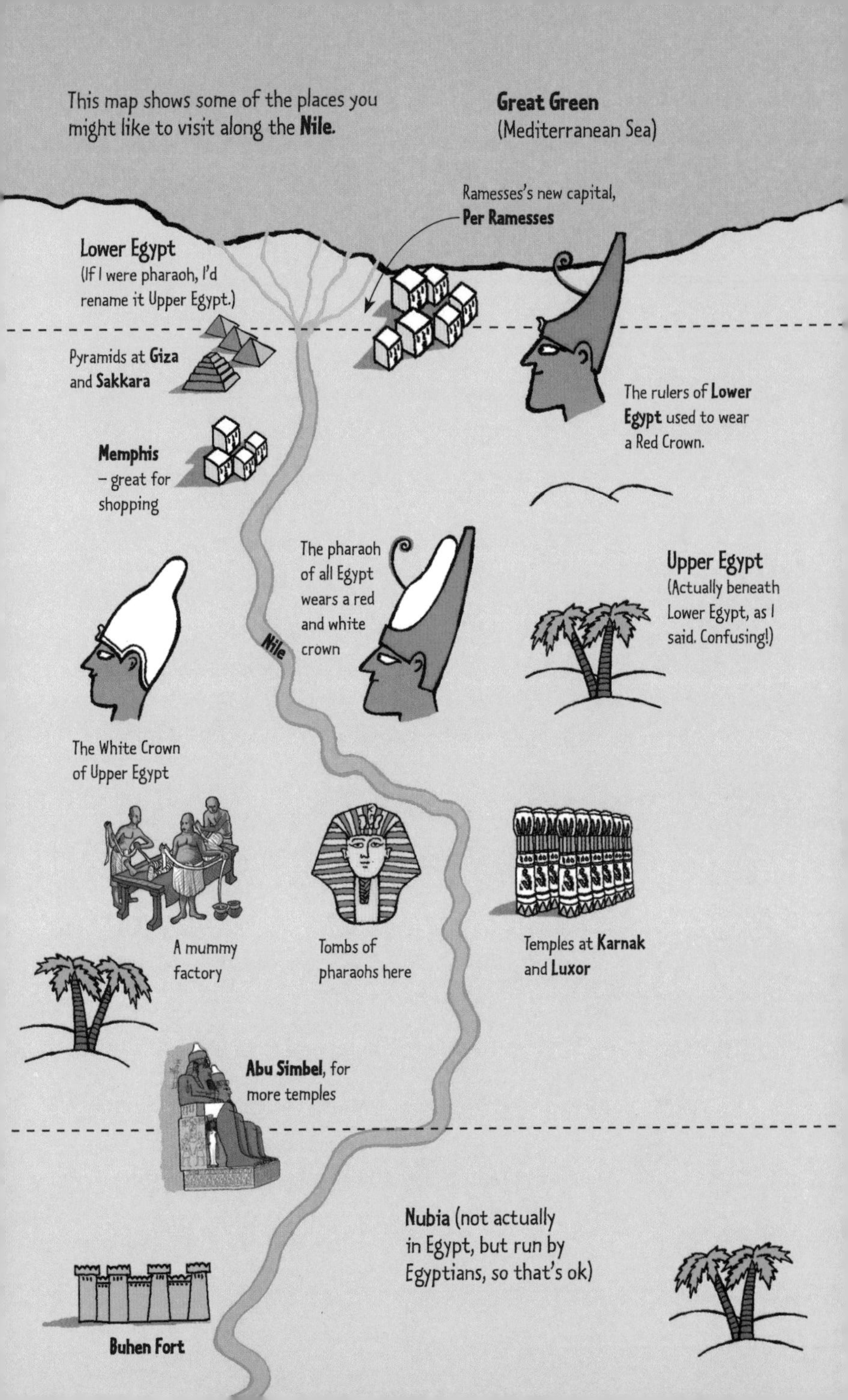
This map shows some of the places you might like to visit along the **Nile.**
Great Green (Mediterranean Sea)
Ramesses's new capital, **Per Ramesses**
Lower Egypt (If I were pharaoh, I'd rename it Upper Egypt.)
Pyramids at **Giza** and **Sakkara**
The rulers of **Lower Egypt** used to wear a Red Crown.
Memphis – great for shopping
The pharaoh of all Egypt wears a red and white crown
Upper Egypt (Actually beneath Lower Egypt, as I said. Confusing!)
Nile
The White Crown of Upper Egypt
A mummy factory
Tombs of pharaohs here
Temples at **Karnak** and **Luxor**
Abu Simbel, for more temples
Nubia (not actually in Egypt, but run by Egyptians, so that's ok)
Buhen Fort

The best linen is thin and slightly see-through. So don't forget to wear a loincloth underneath.

What not to wear

This kind of party frock was worn in the past, but now it's hopelessly out of fashion. So, if you're a girl, avoid the beaded look if you want to fit in.

Party wig

The dress was covered with hundreds of different beads.

Decorative beads

What to wear

Buy some light, loose linen tunics when you arrive - the markets are easy to find, just follow the shouting and the smell of donkeys. Buy quite a few, so you can change each time you get sweaty.

Egyptian fashions change veeerrrry slowly and it can take centuries for a new look to emerge. But, as a guide, looks like the ones below are SO this century... or maybe last, but that's fine too.

For men, a skirt and pleated robes are great party wear.

For women, fine linen dresses and shawls are trendy.

If you're a boy, you'd better get used to wearing a skirt (known as a kilt). Over that, anyone who's anyone wears pleated linen robes tied with a sash. Girls should go for a pleated dress with a shawl, and perhaps a headband to finish off the look.

Foreign fashions?

If you don't fancy Egyptian fashion, you could always try to pass your modern outfits off as some outlandish foreign style: "This is what everyone wears in Outer Farawayland!" you could say.

But, to be honest, that wouldn't get you far in Egypt. To fit in with polite society and avoid being treated like a foreign weirdo, you should try to look and act as Egyptian as possible.

Hairstyles and wigs

While you should keep it simple with your clothes, you can go to town with your hair. Or rather, you can go to town in somebody else's hair: wigs are all the rage. Ask around for a wig stall at the first market you visit.

Girls of all ages can try out luxuriously curled and tousled locks, strung with gold strands, flowers, tassels and beads. Boys should shave all but a 'sidelock' of hair, while men wear plain-ish wigs. Some people (even women) shave their heads under their wigs to stay cool.

> ### Top tips for tourists
>
> Nº 2: The naked look
>
> Very young visitors would blend in best if they don't wear anything at all, but only those younger than six.
>
> If you're a boy, you'll also have to shave your hair. But remember to keep enough for the sidelock. That's a braid on the side of the head – like a ponytail that's lost its way.

Trendy hair (or rather wig) styles

Woman

Man

Little boy

Sandals made out of papyrus – a type of reed that grows by the Nile – are cheap and sturdy.

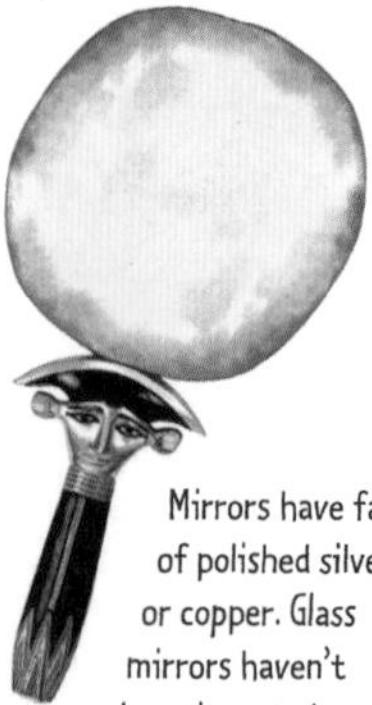

Mirrors have faces of polished silver or copper. Glass mirrors haven't been invented yet.

You could buy a pretty box like this from a market to store your eyeliner – and that means you too, boys.

Fancy footwear

Egyptians go barefoot indoors, but they wear sandals in the dirty, dusty streets. Make sure you pick up a sturdy pair from a market. You don't want them to fall apart before you've walked home.

Royalty often have theirs decorated with gold, but simple papyrus (a type of reed) or leather sandals are just fine for mere mortals. If you're going to a party, though (see pages 94-95) you might want to pick up a more decorative pair.

Men in make-up

Ancient Egyptians aren't into equal opportunities all of the time, but they are when it comes to make-up. Both women *and* men wear thick, dramatic eyeliner and other perfumed cosmetics.

It's not just about looks, though; the thick eyeliner paint protects the eyes from flies. Various oils are also used on the face, to protect the skin from the fierce sun. You might want to bring your own sunscreen and put that on first to be safe. Pick the wrong oil and you might end up cooking yourself instead of protecting your skin.

Every day is wash day

I can't stress enough how important it is to keep clean in Egypt. Egyptians always wash in the morning and before main meals. But I'd fit in as many showers as you have time for to be on the safe side. (See the box on page 26 for where and how to have a shower.)

There's no soap, but the markets sell lots of cleansing creams made from perfume, oil and lime. If you shave your head, you can just slap on a wig, but if you decide to keep your own hair, you can buy many hair cleaning lotions - even anti-dandruff ones.

Top tips for tourists

№ 3: Try the perfume

Egyptian perfumes are famous throughout the ancient world, and would make a great gift to take back home.

The best are made from frankincense and myrrh – remember, the gifts given to baby Jesus? – and fragrant plants from Arabia and East Africa.

The finishing touches

When you've bought your robes, scrubbed yourself clean and put on eyeliner, it's time to complete your Egyptian outfit with some fancy trinkets. You'd need to visit a market in a classier part of town for these.

Some necklaces are so hefty they're actually more like collars. It might be a good idea to do some neck-strengthening exercises before you go.

If you have pierced ears, big earrings are in fashion.

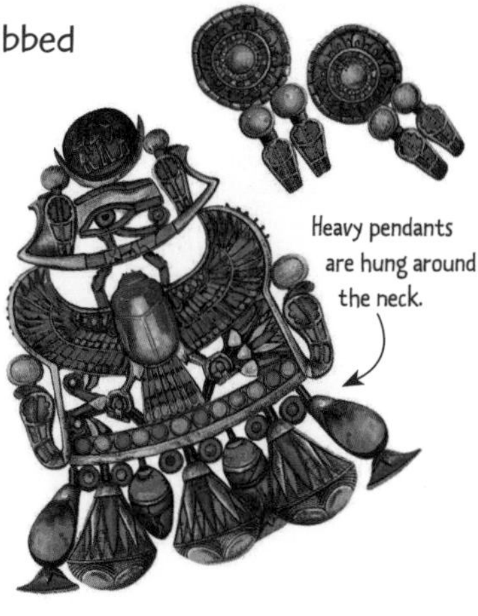

Heavy pendants are hung around the neck.

Where do you fit in?

Life at the top isn't always easy. As a living god, if the harvest fails, the blame rests solely on the shoulders of the pharaoh.

Social rank is very important in Ancient Egypt, so you'll need to familiarize yourself with who fits in where so you don't make embarassing blunders. Treating a high priest like a peasant will *not* make you popular.

So, who should you look up to? Who do you get to boss around? Look at the diagram on the right. You see the scribes? They're professional writers, and fairly high up the social ladder. Sadly, you're WAY below them. What about priests and doctors? You're below them too. As a foreigner, you're roughly between soldiers and peasants. Many people you meet will be polite and friendly but if you throw your weight around, you'll soon be put in your place.

A fair(ish) trial

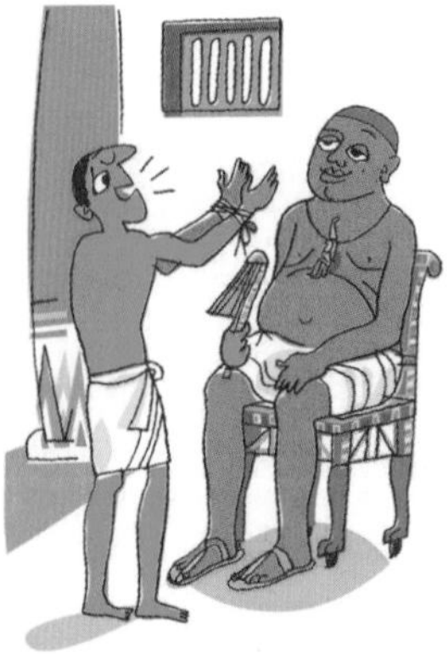

Anyone accused of a crime is allowed to defend himself in court. A bit of flattery sent the judge's way never hurts.

If you're accused of a crime, you'll get the same treatment as a local, though. For example, if you were found guilty of stealing, you'd have to repay what you stole.

But woe betide anyone who steals from a palace, a temple, or the pharaoh. (Maybe I shouldn't say what'd happen if you did that, in case I frighten more sensitive readers?)

A pyramid of people showing the structure of Egyptian society

Viziers are chief advisers to the pharaoh. One is in charge of Upper Egypt, and the other Lower Egypt.

Mayors and governors are the big cheeses of town life.

Even within classes, there's a definite order. Scribes can be anything from letter writers to government officials.

Upwardly mobile

It's not unheard of for a peasant family to rise from the ranks: but it usually takes a few generations.

If a peasant girl gets a job as a handmaid and earns enough to send her son to school, he could become a scribe. Then his son might be able to go even further.

Meet the pharaoh

Top tips for tourists

№ 4: Kingly gifts

Suitable gifts to give to the pharaoh include: perfumes, ostrich eggs, baboons, gold and beautiful women. Although most Egyptian men just marry one woman, pharaohs have many wives and are often looking for more.

Although you're just a lowly foreigner, you'll be welcome almost anywhere in Egypt if you come bearing gifts. You might even get an audience with the pharaoh if you bring him enough lovely pressies. The pharaoh's latest, greatest palace is in Per Ramesses, so it's worth checking if he's there when you're in town. But how do you get to see him?

Well, ambassadors from countries that Egypt has conquered are always bringing the pharaoh 'gifts' - though these presents are more like a tax they have to pay for the privilege of being beaten in battle.

So, load up on fancy goods, dress up in even fancier robes, and roll up to the pharaoh's palace in the guise of an ambassador from a foreign land.

Scrub up nicely

The pharaoh's servants wash him many times a day. So you have high standards to live up to.

Don't even think about going to meet the pharaoh without washing carefully. If you think you're clean enough... then you should probably wash again all over just to make sure. Once you're squeaky clean and dressed up to the nines, you're ready to enter the presence of a living god.

Kneel before god

Remember, the pharaoh is actually a living god, so make extra sure to mind your manners. Gods don't take kindly to mortals who don't show the proper respect.

Here are some divine-wrath-avoidance tips:

1) When you enter the pharaoh's presence, bow so that your nose rubs in the dust. Repeat six more times.

2) Ply the pharaoh with luxurious presents - gold and jewels are good, though exotic wild animals are also a good choice.

3) Don't stare. Gods don't like that. Back away slowly and respectfully after a while.

4) Once you're safely in the crowd you can goggle at the magnificent pharaoh to your heart's content. Though if he looks displeased with your present, leave by the closest available exit.

Long live the palace!

Pharaohs are so important that people aren't supposed to refer to them by name.

So, just talk about 'the pharaoh'. The word pharaoh comes from the Egyptian for 'palace', *per-aa*, so you're actually talking about the king as though he's a building.

"So, what else have you brought me, foreign wretch?"

Who you gonna call?

If you're the victim of a crime - or if you're being chased by thugs who make you feel you're *about* to be a victim any second now - you can ask the *Medjay* (the Egyptian police) for help.

They're a reasonable bunch, on the whole, but they sometimes need some encouragement (see left) to get the job done quickly.

Local police use snuffling sniffer dogs to track down criminals.

Greasing the wheels

Learning how to deal with the local police is vital if you find yourself in need of their help.

Let's just say, my stolen luggage turned up the morning after I'd treated a policeman to a piping hot meal and fine jug of wine. You might find they're eager to help if you offer a similar gift.

Think of it as a charitable donation – the police are badly paid here.

Weights and measures

When buying food at the market, you'll need to know how things are measured. The basic weight is a *deben*, which weighs about the same as a large egg. Length is measured in cubits - the distance from a man's elbow to his finger tips.

Length is usually measured using people's arms and hands. Obviously this means lengths can sometimes vary.

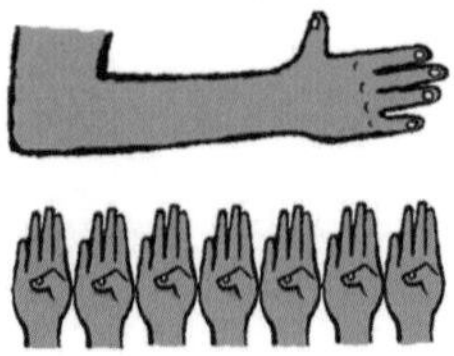

For smaller measurements, spans (hands) or digits (fingers) are used. Seven spans or 28 digits make a cubit.

Telling the time

Egyptians don't have clocks, which means no one can nag you for being five minutes late, because five minutes doesn't exist. Time's measured roughly, using the Sun.

If your ship leaves at daybreak, then be on the jetty as the Sun begins to rise. If it leaves at midday, be there as the Sun hangs high in the sky; and if it leaves at dusk, then make sure you're standing with your bags at your feet as the Sun sinks below the horizon. Simple, right?

Top tips for tourists

Nº 5: Little trickster

A notorious trader's trick is hiring someone with short arms to measure their wares.

When shopping, demand to have your goods measured in Royal Cubits (52.5cm or 21 in), using a stick, as these never change. If they refuse, threaten to get the *Medjay* involved. They should shape up quickly.

What day is it?

The official calendar marks twelve 30-day months, plus five holy days stuck on the end. It's not particularly complicated, but if you've booked your return ship in advance, double-check the date.

The year is split into three seasons to match the farming cycle. The Nile flood (roughly July to October), growing season (November to February) and summer (March to June). Growing season is the best time to visit, when it's coolest and the towns are quietest.

The Nile floods, spilling over its banks once a year. Egyptians plan their lives around this.

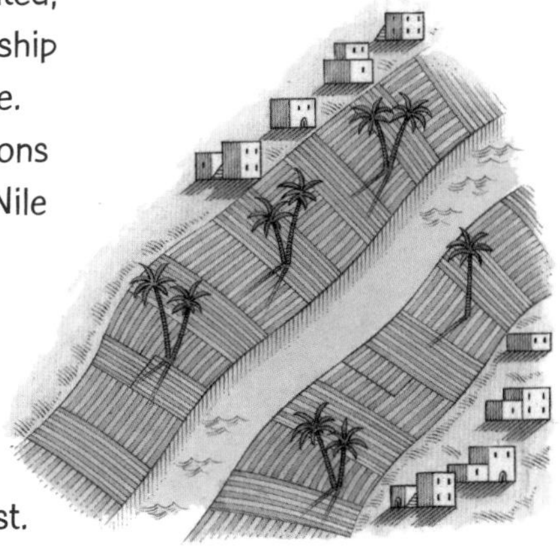

Top tips for tourists

№ 6: Feeling lost?

It's easy to get lost in the dark and winding passageways of Egyptian towns.

The lack of street names doesn't help either. Your best hope of finding your way around is to memorize local landmarks.

Where to stay

For much of your trip, you'll be taking boat trips and sleeping in a cabin on board, or on the riverbank. But it's definitely worth sticking around in towns such as Per Ramesses and Memphis for a while. That's where you'll get to see everyday Egyptian life in all its hot, noisy, bustling glory.

But where to stay? You *could* get a bed in an inn... but you'd also get thieves, bed-bugs and drunken louts. The solution? Rent a house. (Town houses are cheapest.)

This is a scene typical of any of the large towns you'll visit.

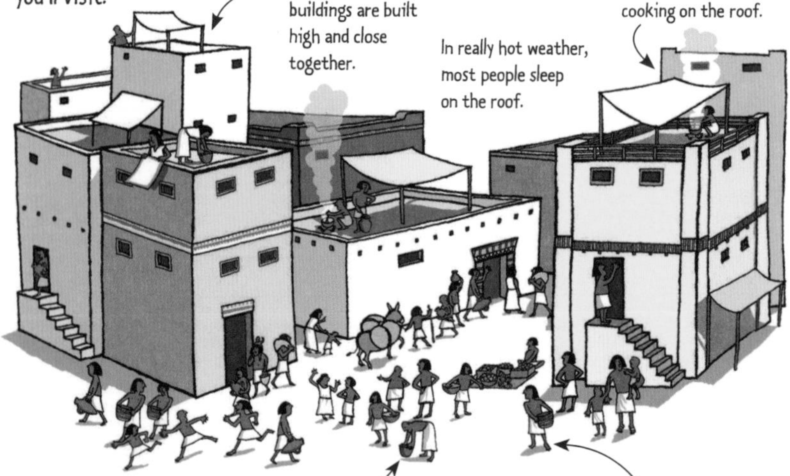

Space is hard to come by, so buildings are built high and close together.
In really hot weather, most people sleep on the roof.
Because of the heat, Egyptians do their cooking on the roof.
Phew! Carrying home heavy shopping is hard work.
Bring a basket to carry bread.

Luxury accommodation

Key

1. The central room
2. The garden
3. The bedrooms
4. Stables
5. Storage
6. Pool

If you've got a good price for the pepper you brought with you, you might be able to afford to rent the villa (large house) of a minor official.

These overworked pen-pushers spend a lot of time away from home, so they rent out their villas to make some quick cash (well, copper weights). Villas come with servants and - if you're lucky - a horse and chariot in the stable.

This is what your villa will probably look like: (The roof's cut away so you can look in.)

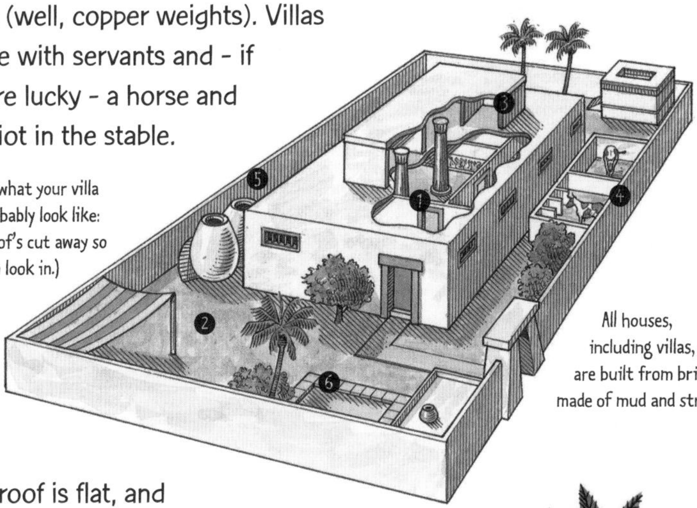

All houses, including villas, are built from bricks made of mud and straw.

The roof is flat, and that's where people go to escape the heat - they might even sleep up there. If your house is in the middle of a town, it'll give you a good view of the streets below. You can see all kinds of street life, from oiled acrobats and Nubian dancers to chanting priests.

Palm trees make some welcome shade in gardens.

Bathroom break

Flushing toilets haven't been invented yet - most bathrooms have a wooden or stone seat with a hole in the middle instead. This is placed over a clay container filled with sand, and it's up to you to add more sand after you've finished. (This keeps the smells in.)

On the whole, Egyptian toilets aren't too bad at all. But, as Egyptians are so picky about cleanliness, any household that forgets to empty its clay pot is in for a rough time with the people next door.

Shower time

If you like a shower, you'll have to tip a bowl of warm water over your head, as there's no running water. Because of this, the bathrooms in most villas are lined with splash-proof limestone. Villas also come with servants who'll happily take over the pouring duties.

But if you want a taste of how most Egyptians live, join the masses for a morning dip in the Nile.

Home comforts

As you'd imagine, poor people's houses are pretty bare, with perhaps a few stools and a table on the gritty mud floor. But the rich have tiles to cool their soles, and painted chests to keep their secrets.

And what about the beds? Well, if anyone offers you a 'headrest' for your bed, refuse politely: they're made of wood. Luckily, most houses will have at least a few cushions you could use as pillows, and luxury villas will have loads.

The house you rent should have a plentiful supply of linen sheets and covers, so you won't need a sleeping bag.

Hidden treasures

But you won't want to spend much time holed up in your lodgings, so perhaps the lack of creature comforts won't matter much.

When you've unpacked, why not go for a wander through the streets? You'll meet some amazing people and see some strange sights - from beggars with stories of vengeful gods, to graveyards filled with dead cats... it's all there to be stumbled upon.

The backstreets give an authentic glimpse of life in the towns.

Roughing it

If you're the outdoorsy type, you could try camping by the side of the Nile. Egypt by night is extraordinarily beautiful, and you'll be lulled to sleep by the sound of soft water stirring and crickets chirping - and you've never seen so many stars!

It would be irresponsible of me not to warn you, though: you might also meet some curious crocodiles. So avoid camping alone, and hire a local guide to help you stay safe (see right).

Top tips for tourists

№ 7: Happy camping

Local guides will take you to a safe spot to camp, and provide you with tents. They'll also light a fire to keep you warm and throw on sweet-smelling herbs to keep the mosquitoes at bay.

Getting around

Top tips
for tourists

Nº 8: Striking a deal

If a cheeky ferryman asks for more than two copper weights, scowl and turn away in disgust.

He may drop his price. But, more importantly, the other ferrymen will see you're no mug and will offer a fair deal.

There aren't any roads to speak of in Egypt, so the only real 'highway' is the River Nile, which snakes its way right down the middle of the country. It begins its journey in the great lakes of central Africa, and makes its way past jungles and swamps, before flowing into Egypt and cutting the desert in two.

It's swarming with boats that can offer you a lift for a small fee, from ferries to barges laden with grain (watch out for rats). It's really the only way to get around.

Ferrymen ply their trade between the east and west banks, and should charge no more than a couple of small copper weights for a ride.

From dawn until dusk, the river is crowded with every type of craft.

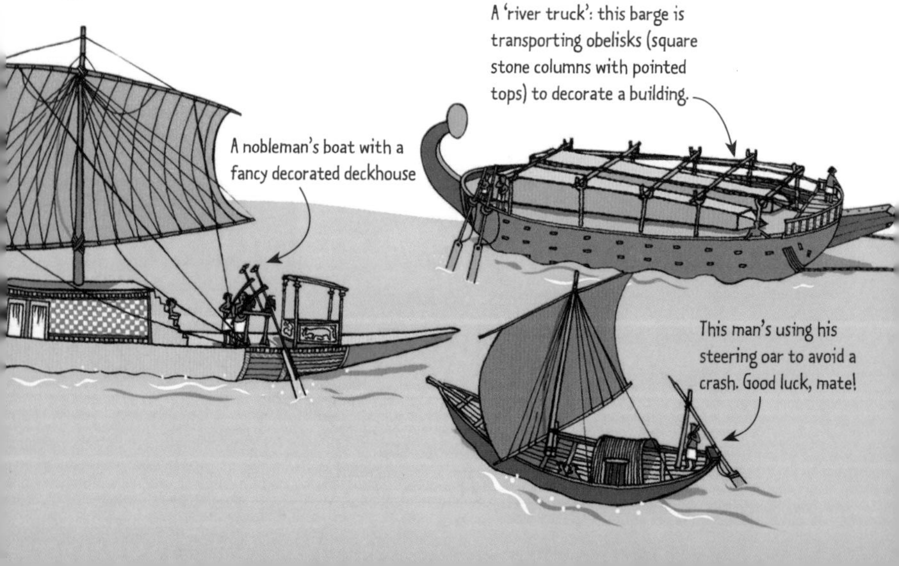

A 'river truck': this barge is transporting obelisks (square stone columns with pointed tops) to decorate a building.
A nobleman's boat with a fancy decorated deckhouse
This man's using his steering oar to avoid a crash. Good luck, mate!

A river cruise

For a longer trip on the Nile, jump on a boat heading south. Savvy adventurers pick a boat with a canopy, so they can lie in its shade while the blazing green fields slip by. In the evening, the boats moor by the riverbank and most people disembark to eat and sleep.

Away from the town lights, thousands of stars shimmer in the night sky. But don't get too carried away with looking up and wander away from camp. Hungry crocodiles could be lurking - and they won't be gazing at the stars... they'll be more interested in your ankles.

Get your bearings

Look for boats with sails. The current flows north, while the wind tends to blow against the current, to the south.

So, boats going south need sails AND oars, but north-bound ones just use oars. This inspired the Egyptians' picture writing symbols for 'south' and 'north'. (More on picture writing later.)

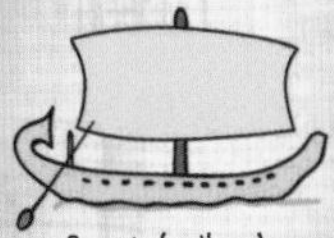

South (sail up)

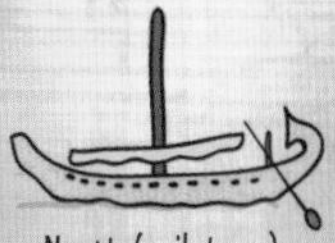

North (sail down)

Crocodiles are a danger. You might want to pray to Sobek, the crocodile god, for a safe trip.

An official in a hurry

"Come on boys, put your back in to it!"

A landowner on a sailing boat trip with his family

Not wheely useful

In the towns, you might find a chariot to rent, pulled by a horse.

But the distances in town are so small that it's hardly worth the hassle of hiring one.

Plus, I reckon you get a better feel for a town by strolling around and taking it all in slowly.

Slow going

Getting about by land is tricky, as there aren't any roads between towns. There wouldn't be any point, as they'd be washed away by the Nile floods each year.

There aren't even any camels, either. (There won't be any in Egypt for about 700 years.) Horses are an option, but only for the very rich. Donkeys are the standard beast of burden, though they're more likely to be used to carry your stuff than you.

Carrying chairs are available in towns, but they always make me feel a bit of a lemon, perched above everyone's heads, trying to look nonchalant, while secretly praying your bearers don't slip and send you tumbling in a red-faced heap.

Top tips for tourists

Nº 9: Desert storm

NEVER agree to a tour of the desert with a friendly 'guide'. You could well be robbed and left for dead. And if you're lucky enough to escape with your life, there's a good chance you'll lose your way coming back.

One Persian general lost his entire army in the desert and it was never seen again.

Deadly deserts

If you venture far from the towns, you'll need a string of donkeys carrying plenty of water. Dehydration and heat exhaustion are constant threats, and you won't go far in the desert without coming across the whitened bones of some unlucky animal.

To avoid meeting a similar fate, there are a few things you need to bear in mind.

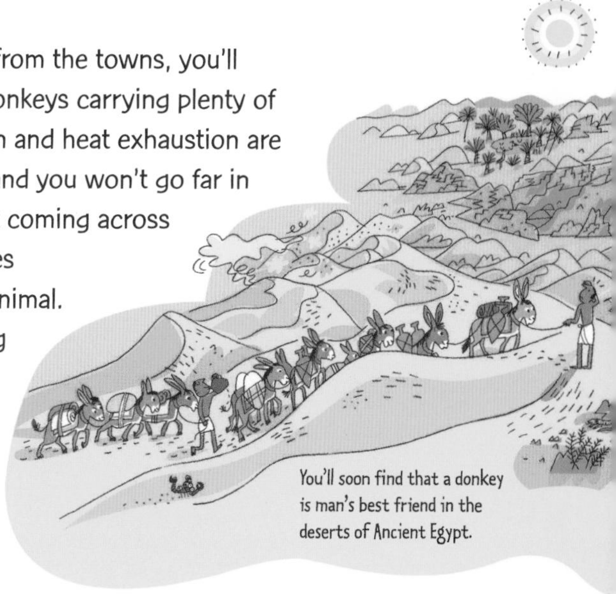

You'll soon find that a donkey is man's best friend in the deserts of Ancient Egypt.

Safety tips

If you venture far into the desert, remember: this can be bandit country.

Egyptians call it the *deshret*, which means 'red land'. Red symbolizes chaos in Ancient Egypt, so as you can imagine, it's no picnic spot.

Latching onto a group of traders is your only safe option. They know how to defend themselves, and, crucially, where to find water in wells and pools in the desert known as oases.

In the desert, a bandit attack could happen at any time.

Pigeons are fattened for the table. (Watch out for bones.)

Top tips for tourists

Nº 10: Eating out is out

Food-lovers are well catered for in Ancient Egypt, but if you like to eat out, you're out of luck.

There are no cafés, and only a few snack bars and inns, serving bread, meat and beer.

Proud Egyptians like to boast about the quality of their wine.

Food & drink

One sad fact I have to break to you right away is that Ancient Egypt has no chocolate. By all means take some with you, but don't give any to the locals, or they'll start wondering why they've never had any before. Perhaps the pharaoh is keeping it all to himself? Revolutions, riots, and mass hysteria will surely follow. On second thoughts, maybe you should just leave the chocolate at home; it'll just melt anyway.

Self-catering vs eating out

Eating out is a problem, as restaurants haven't been invented yet. You might find the odd stall where you can buy a cooked meal, but don't count on it. If you hate cooking - or, like me, the only thing you can make in the kitchen is a mess - you can hire servants to do it for you. (If you're staying in a villa, you'll get them for free.)

It's worth buying your own ingredients, though, as it gives you a chance to wander around the market and interact with some locals - even if it is just in sign language. So, head down to the nearest market and get shopping.

At the market

You'll always find a fish stall piled with fresh fish and stacks of dried fish (which keeps longer and smells less).

There'll also be bakers selling all kinds of bread, from flat breads to loaves made with spices, honey and seeds. "FRESH FROM THE OVEN," they bellow, with hands covered in flour. (What they won't tell you is that the loaves may contain grit because they're made outdoors. So chew with care, or risk losing a tooth.)

Meat and veg

You can buy all kinds of meats, from lamb and mutton to duck or juicy pork - even a nice piece of goat meat if you're feeling adventurous. Beef's only for special occasions, as it's very expensive, and cows are kept mainly for milk and cheese.

You're out of luck if you only eat chicken, as they're very rare - so rare, in fact, that the pharaoh exhibits just a handful of them in his private zoo. And I don't think he'd like you eating them.

Fruit and vegetables grow in abundance, though, so you won't go short of those.

Spoilt for choice

At the market, you can pick up everything from dates, lentils and pomegranates to meat, eggs, nuts and cheese. (I copied the picture below from an Egyptian sign, so I'm not *quite* sure what it all is.)

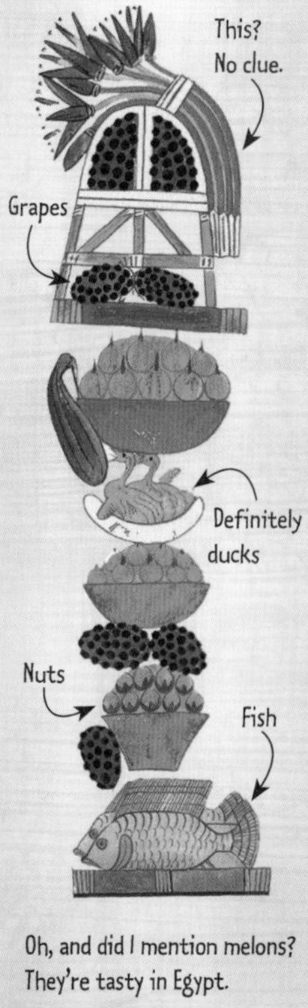

Oh, and did I mention melons? They're tasty in Egypt.

Cheers!

Beer is drunk through a filter. But even after straining, it's still full of lumps.

There aren't any fizzy drinks or cartons of juice to be had, but it's (usually) safe to drink water from the Nile, and there are wells that you can use too. If you're in a villa, you could always get a servant to squeeze you some fresh fruit juice for a change.

One typical Egyptian drink is lumpy beer. This looks alarming, but it's strangely popular. It's made from crumbled bread and water and doesn't contain much alcohol.

Apparently it tastes nice enough, but I think I'd rather take someone else's word for it than take the risk myself.

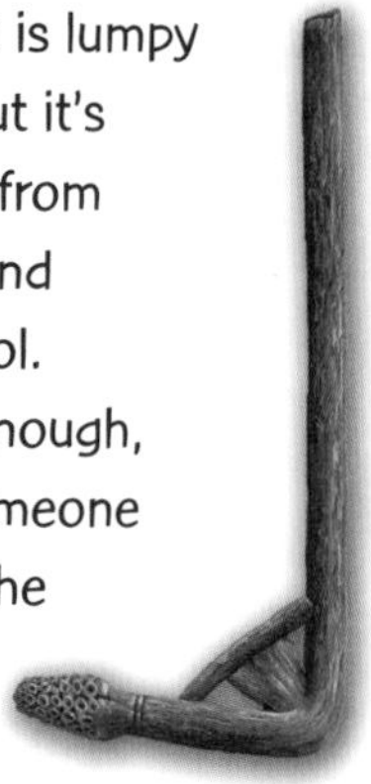

A drinking straw

Don't try this at home

Wherever you are in Egypt, you'll see women balancing enormous baskets on their head. It's a skill that takes years of practice, so leave it to the experts.

The perfect gift

The wine is said to be excellent, especially a variety called *Shedeh*. Made from red grapes, this warm, spiced wine helps the rich take the chill off winter nights. It's graced royal banquets for as long as anyone can remember. You'll be lucky to find any in the marketplace, but if you do, it would make a great gift for somebody back home.

Cooking outdoors

All the cooking is done outside or on the roof, to keep houses cool, and to avoid burning them to the ground. Think of it as a barbecue on the beach, complete with sand in the wind, and flies fighting past a forest of swatting arms.

Cook like an Egyptian

Only women bake their own bread. If you're male, you'll get funny looks if you do it.

Most Egyptians cook on a tripod (three-legged stand) over a fire.

To keep a fire going, you'll have to fan the flames. (And it helps if somebody fans you at the same time.)

Loaves are stuck on the outside of an oven (the inside's for the fire). They fall off when they're cooked.

Fan the flames

If you're cooking for yourself, you'll have to go back to basics. Everything's cooked on charcoal or using fire of some kind. Common fuels include sticks, dry grass and reeds. Reeds give bursts of heat but need constant fanning to keep alight. (This is where servants come in handy.)

> *“It feels as though I've been slaving over this blaze since the world began.”*
>
> A hot and bothered Egyptian cook

Mix and match

Many tourists find Egyptian gods a little confusing. There are hundreds, and they often seem to overlap or turn into each other.

For example, at every sunset, the Sun god Re 'becomes' Osiris, the god of the dead. Gods can even join up into new ones. For example, Amun-Re is made up of a god called Amun and a god called Re. The land of the gods must get rather crowded...

This is Thoth, the ibis-headed god of scribes, wisdom and the moon. (He has a moon on his head here.)

Gods and goddesses

Perhaps you're wondering why you need to know about Egyptian gods and goddesses as a tourist? After all, they're not real, so it's not as though you'll see any, will you?

Well, no. (Or, probably not.) But knowing about the gods will help you understand how the locals tick. They have a lot of gods and take them very seriously, so you'll blend in a lot better if you at least pretend to do the same. For example, avoid pointing and laughing at pictures of the gods, even if they do look like freaky animal-headed mutants.

You will be the only one laughing... and not for long. (Not unless you find being chased out of a temple by an angry priest really hilarious. Temple priests can run surprisingly fast, I discovered.)

Holy animals

You'll see lots of images of gods with animal heads in temples. This is because Egyptians believe their gods can send part of their spirit into the body of a sacred animal that fits their personal godly quality. So, a sky god might take over a bird, or a fierce-tempered goddess, a lion.

A very Egyptian obsession

In some ways, the lives of the gods are like a more dramatic, soap-opera-y version of life on Earth. They get married, have children, quarrel, scheme... and even die.

That brings me to a part of Egyptian life that you might find strange: their obsession with death. It's not that they're morbid, they just want to make sure their 'next life', or 'afterlife', is as fun as possible, and that takes lots of preparation and planning.

This is especially true of pharaohs, who'll start building their tombs well before they've even got their first wrinkle. (You'll be able to visit some of their tombs on your travels.)

Top tips for tourists

Nº 11: Don't mention his name...

Only once, under King ~~Akhenaten~~, did Egypt almost become a one-god nation.

He promoted a sun god, ~~Aten~~, above all others, but his scheme ended with his reign. ~~Akhenaten~~'s reputation is now so low that the penalty for even saying his name is severe.

Help, mummy!

Speaking of tombs, I should probably bring up mummies at this point. You've probably heard of these bandaged-up bodies before. But why do Egyptians wrap up dead people like that?

It's to preserve the body forever, so the person can use it in his next life. Osiris, the boss god of the dead, was the first to do this. He was murdered, then mummified, which cured his nasty case of death completely.

The god Osiris isn't about to vomit. He just has green skin.

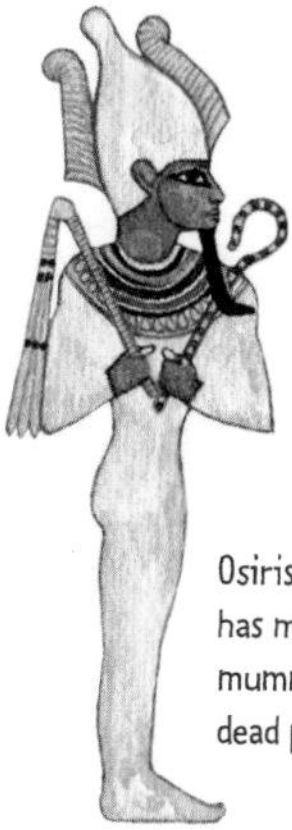

Osiris has made mummies dead popular.

Holy cures

If you fall ill in Ancient Egypt, you'd better pray you get better – literally.

The Egyptians believe that the gods – and their priests – play a powerful role in making you better when you're sick.

Luckily, not everything is left to the gods, though. There are plenty of medicines and other more earthly treatments.

Getting sick

If you're going to fall ill anywhere in the ancient world, Egypt isn't a bad place to do it. When one of their family is ill, kings from distant lands wave their hands and stamp their feet. "Where's my Egyptian doctor?" they cry. In fact, no royal court in the world is complete without a physician boasting knowledge from the land of the pharaohs.

Egyptian doctors are often priests and temples provide training. Each temple has its own speciality, so if you've been stung by a scorpion, you should visit the priests at the temples of the goddess Selket, who are scorpion specialists. But for the plague, head for the priests of the goddess Sekhmet.

One king brought his entire family over from a country called Canaan, just to consult an Egyptian doctor.

Local doctors

Not all doctors are priests, though. Local, non-holy doctors can be found in most Egyptian towns. Each will have his own area of expertise - or claim to - but if he's worth his salt (a common fee) he should be able to treat all the regular ailments.

Mind you, cures can be hit and miss, and Egyptian doctors can have some peculiar ideas. I went to see one for indigestion. He gave me honey cakes with a sprinkling of pig's tooth. It didn't do any good - I was lucky it didn't give me *extra* indigestion.

Top tips for tourists

Nº 12: DIY healing

You could always pray directly to a god associated with healing, such as Isis, Sekhmet or Imhotep by leaving a *stela* (stone with a prayer on) at a temple.

Some are covered in ears, to remind the gods to listen to the prayers.

Gulp! Surgery

If you urgently need an operation, your chances of survival are actually fairly high - for the ancient world, at least. Instruments are sterilized in flame and surgeons keep both their patients and surroundings very clean. There's even a painkiller made from poppies.

But 3,500 year-old surgery has its limits. If the operation can wait until you get home, I strongly recommend it.

A pair of iron tweezers

This knife is used in surgery. It may not look it, but it's very sharp.

"Lovely mud this time of year, I must say."

A Nile mud bath

If you see someone sitting by the Nile, covered in mud, don't point or laugh. A Nile mud bath is a popular treatment for skin infections. (Hmm, the thought of other people's scabby skin doesn't make me keen to swim in the Nile, mind you.)

> *"O... Isis... come and see your father concerning that enemy, dead man or dead woman, which is in the head of this man..."*
>
> A charm for curing a headache caused by a spirit inside the head

The right frame of mind

Although I said not all doctors are priests, do bear in mind that all treatment involves prayer. This doesn't mean the doctors are quacks, just that Egyptians find faith and hope to be great healers. But you don't have to believe to get the benefits from their herbal remedies or surgical skills.

If the doctors can't help, they'll prescribe a nap in the temple grounds, in the hope that the god will offer a cure.

Gods can show people how to get better in their dreams.

You can buy anti-illness charms at the market.

Part two:

Into Upper Egypt

When you first arrive, you might like to spend a little time in the capital, Per Ramesses. But once you've had a look around, got your bearings, and maybe even met the pharaoh, it's time to find a boat and begin your Nile tour.

Giza should be your first stop, for the great pyramids. Then, head on to Memphis, Heliopolis and Sakkara for more adventures.

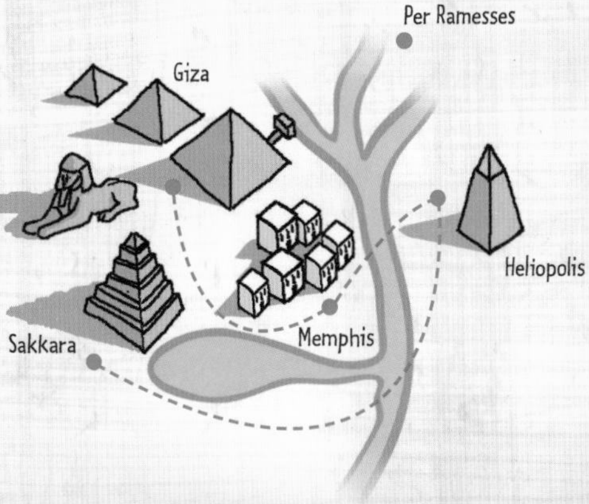

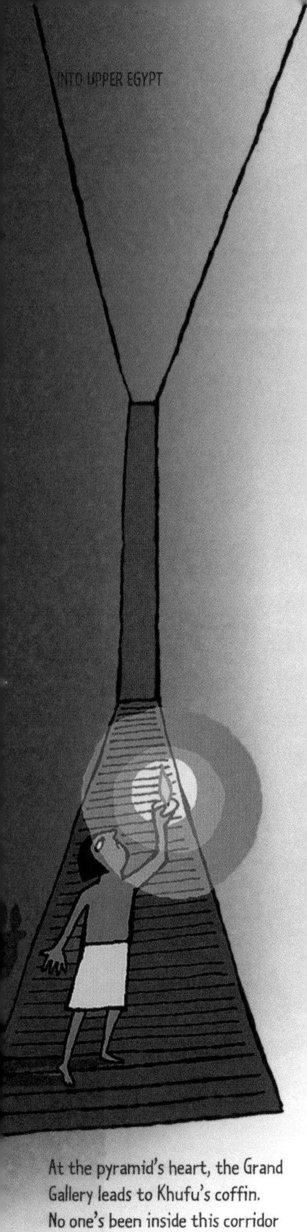

At the pyramid's heart, the Grand Gallery leads to Khufu's coffin. No one's been inside this corridor for over a thousand years. (Apart from in this picture, but that's just the artist taking liberties.)

A touristy graveyard

The first stop I suggest making is at the breathtaking Giza pyramids. Rising from the desert, these grand, ancient monuments will already be over a thousand years old by the time of your visit.

But what are they for? Think of them as a royal graveyard - the pyramids were built as giant tombs for three pharaohs: Khufu, Khafre and Menkaure.

If you think hanging around people's graves sounds depressing, try to think like an Ancient Egyptian. They don't think death is scary - it's just what you need to do to reach the (usually enjoyable) afterlife. Locals see the pyramids as a jolly day out.

Heavyweight facts

Khufu's pyramid is the largest. At 140m (460ft), it's taller than 24 giraffes; and with more than 2.5 million stone blocks, it weighs nearly twice as much as all the elephants in the world put together.

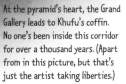

The work force

Each pyramid took about 20 years to build, so it's a good thing the builders weren't being paid by the hour. Most of them were peasants doing *corvée* (work tax), which means they had to work for free. But although they might have to put up with the occasional beating, they only had to stay on the job for a few months.

Plus, they got excellent food for free, and - fingers crossed - the pharaoh might put in a good word for them with the gods in the next life as thanks for building his tomb.

Tools of the trade

These are some of the tools used to cut and shape the stone:

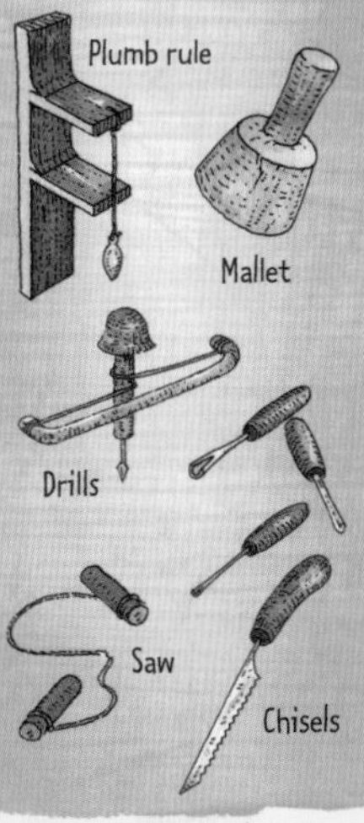

This is how Egyptian historians think the pyramids were built, over 1,000 years before Ramesses's time.

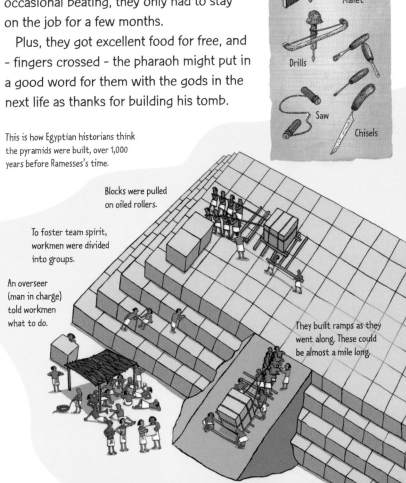

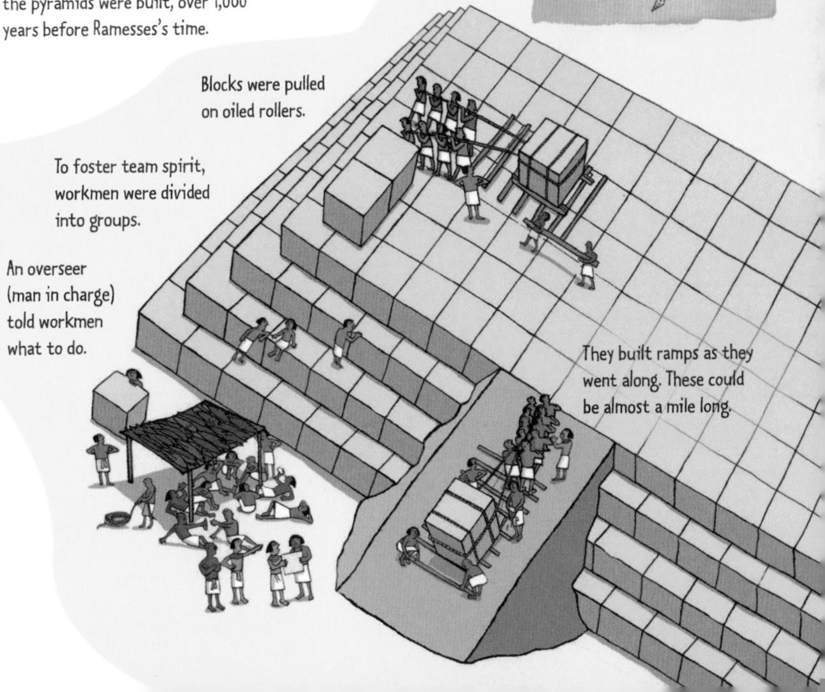

Blocks were pulled on oiled rollers.
To foster team spirit, workmen were divided into groups.
An overseer (man in charge) told workmen what to do.
They built ramps as they went along. These could be almost a mile long.

Top tips
for tourists

№ 13: 100% fake

Don't buy any of the 'genuine pyramid stones' or 'genuine royal jewels' from the souvenir sellers who flock around the pyramids. Firstly, it's illegal. And secondly, they'll be about as genuine as a plastic blow-up pharaoh.

Glorious Giza

If you're lucky enough to be at Giza at sunset, you'll see the vast pyramids looming above you like mountains against a hazy purple sky. It's the sort of sight that makes you want to write poetry. (Don't worry, though, I won't make you read mine.)

Near the pyramids you can see the Sphinx - a giant sculpture of a creature with a lion's body and a man's head. It was built to guard the royal tomb but, over time, it was buried in the desert's shifting sands. Then, in about 1400BC, a prince named Thutmose had a dream as he slept by the half-buried Sphinx: a god (in Sphinx form) told him that if he cleared the sand away, he'd be the next pharaoh.

He ordered his servants to do just that. (Egyptian princes don't get their hands dirty, even if a god tells them to.) And, sure enough, his dream came true.

If you nap beside the Sphinx, you might dream your own destiny. (Or you might just get sand in uncomfortable places.)

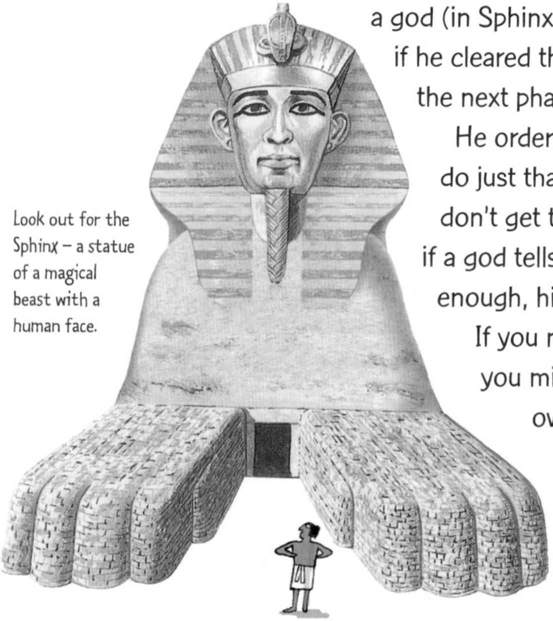

Look out for the Sphinx – a statue of a magical beast with a human face.

Tomb raiders

As I said before, the pyramids are tombs. But they're also treasure stores. Egyptians believe that you get to keep your possessions after you die, so they're buried with everything they might need in the afterlife. For most people, this means clothes, food and the odd trinket. But, for pharaohs, it means whole rooms full of gold and jewels.

To keep out thieves, the pharaohs had their pyramids sealed and placed under heavy guard. They also built empty chambers to fool robbers. Even so, the pyramids were slowly cleared out by daring raiders.

Sneaky pharaohs

Pharaohs tend have their tombs built well in advance of their deaths, to keep their treasure safe in the afterlife.

King Amenemhet III even had a maze-like series of secret passageways, trap doors and dead ends in his, around his burial chamber. But raiders still robbed him blind, so presumably the pharaoh spent the rest of his afterlife feeling poor.

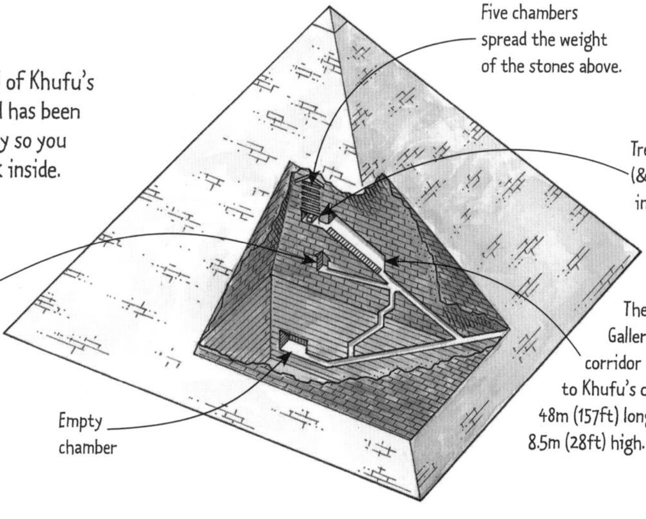

Five chambers spread the weight of the stones above.
The wall of Khufu's pyramid has been cut away so you can look inside.
Treasure (& Khufu) in here
Empty chamber
The Grand Gallery: a corridor leading to Khufu's chamber. 48m (157ft) long and 8.5m (28ft) high.
Empty chamber

NEXT STOP MEMPHIS
(Beware of pickpockets!)

Marvels of Memphis

> **The old capital**
>
> Memphis was founded by King Menes, Egypt's first ever pharaoh after Upper and Lower Egypt were united. It's still important enough to enjoy regular visits from the pharaoh. So if you don't get a chance to see him in Per Ramesses, pop in on him here. (Don't forget to take gifts.)

A little further along the river, you'll come to Egypt's former capital, Memphis - the city of merchants. If you like shopping, this place is a dream come true. With traders visiting from all over the (known) world, you can pick up exotic goodies, from incense to gold.

But remember to haggle: start the bidding low, and try not to look as though you just got off the boat from the Land of Incredibly Gullible Tourists.

Where Egypt's imports come from

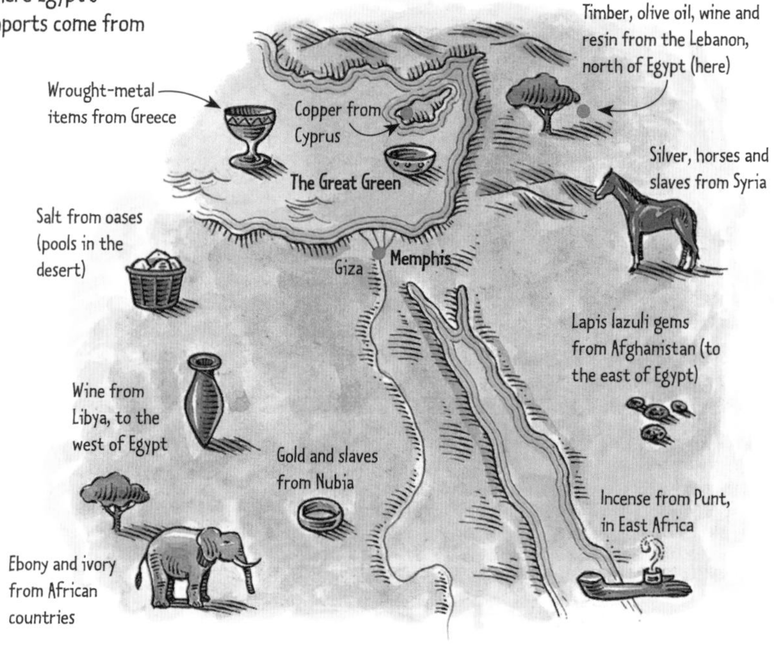

People-watching paradise

In Memphis, the cries of street traders mingle with the babble of soldiers and sailors. Peasants selling blocks of salt move aside for foreign rulers bearing gold tributes for the king. You shouldn't get too many funny looks from the locals here, as there will be foreigners everywhere.

I definitely recommend a visit to the dockyard, where you can see boats being loaded with exports such as papyrus (ancient paper) and linen, and other ships arriving with precious cargoes of cedar wood from nearby Lebanon.

You're also bound to see groups of lively young sailors basking in the sun, playing the popular Egyptian board game, *Senet.*

Top tips for tourists

№ 14: Foiling thieves

Any busy market place is buzzing with thieves. To keep your valuables safe, wear a bag that hangs across your chest.

If a thief still manages to nick it, you'll have to call for the *Medjay*. In Ramesses's time, crime isn't too bad, but you can never be too careful in a busy city like Memphis.

You'll spot people from all over the world in Memphis.

This trader is from nearby Nubia

You can spot Egyptians, as they tend to wear wigs.

The temple of Ptah

The god Ptah created life.

In Memphis, you can see one of the largest temples in Egypt. It's devoted to the local god, Ptah. Most cities have their own deity, but Memphians say that theirs was creator of all things. (Of course, Egyptians visiting from other cities strongly disagree.)

Luckily, Egyptians are a laid-back bunch, so you're unlikely to see fighting in the streets over religion. The rivalry rarely goes beyond snide remarks or sarcastic graffiti.

Still, when in Memphis, I'd be polite about Ptah. For one thing, he lives here. At least, a creature called the Apis bull lives here - and it's supposed to be Ptah in animal form. (It's not always the same bull. When one Apis bull dies, another takes its place.)

Top tips for tourists

Nº 15: Agony uncle

Something worrying you? Visit the Apis bull. This sacred bull will answer any question – as long as the answer is yes or no.

Go to the south of the temple when you see a crowd gather – it means the bull's coming out.

Feeding troughs marked YES and NO are put in front of the bull. When the priest asks your question, the trough the bull eats from gives your answer.

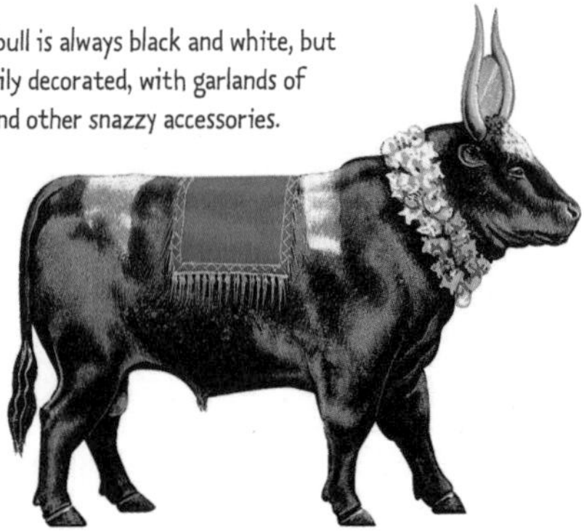

The Apis bull is always black and white, but he's gaudily decorated, with garlands of flowers and other snazzy accessories.

Sun City

The town of Heliopolis - which boasts a temple to Re, the Sun God - is only a short boat ride away.

There are no roofs in the temple to the Sun, so make sure you cover your head and slap on sunscreen if you go in the day.

This temple is at its most magical around sunrise, though, so if you get up early you can get the best view *and* avoid sunstroke. Plus, the markets will be opening as you leave the temple, so you can get there early to bag a bargain.

Locals say that a stone, called the Benben stone, was sent from heaven from the Sun God Re. You'd think a god could come up with a better gift idea than a lump of rock. (It was probably just a meteorite, anyway.)

God's gift (sort of)

Speaking of bargains, watch out for con artists trying to sell you fake relics. I ran into one while admiring a pointy statue known as an obelisk in a temple courtyard. It was capped by a copy of the 'Benben' stone - a gift from Re, apparently. No one could tell me what happened to the original, but one shifty salesman offered me 'the genuine stone' for three bags of pepper. (I'm ashamed to say I bought it.)

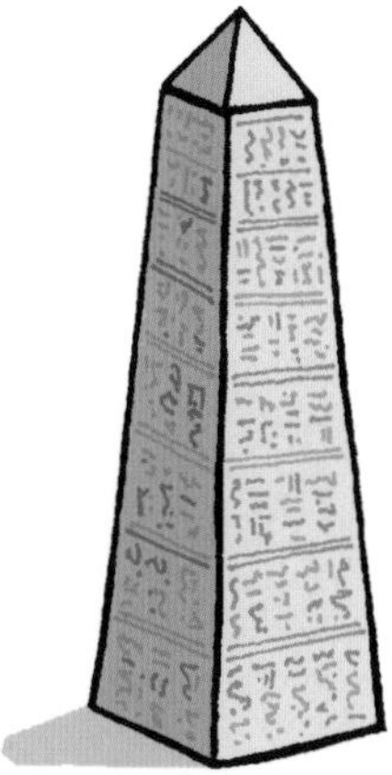

The pointy bit of this temple courtyard obelisk is supposed to be a copy of the Benben stone.

NEXT STOP SAKKARA
(Watch your step!)

City of the dead

Next stop, Sakkara, where you can see something called a necropolis - a fancy cemetery that's basically a whole city built for dead people. Dug into the dusty desert, it houses many powerful people who lived in Memphis long ago, including royalty. But not just people - one tomb is packed with row after row of mummified Apis bulls.

At the necropolis, you can also see the first pyramid ever built. But it doesn't look much like the smooth-sided giants at Giza.

Tomb art

All Egyptian tombs are decorated with paintings and carvings. Many show scenes from everyday life a thousand years before Ramesses II, so it's a bit of a history lesson even for Ancient Egyptians. The carving above shows boat builders hard at work.

This odd-shaped pyramid is very, very ancient indeed.

Many of the buildings are just for show. They look real, but they're completely filled with rubble.

The necropolis is basically a huge model town built for the dead.

The pyramid is set in a vast complex, 547m (1,790ft) by 278m (912ft).

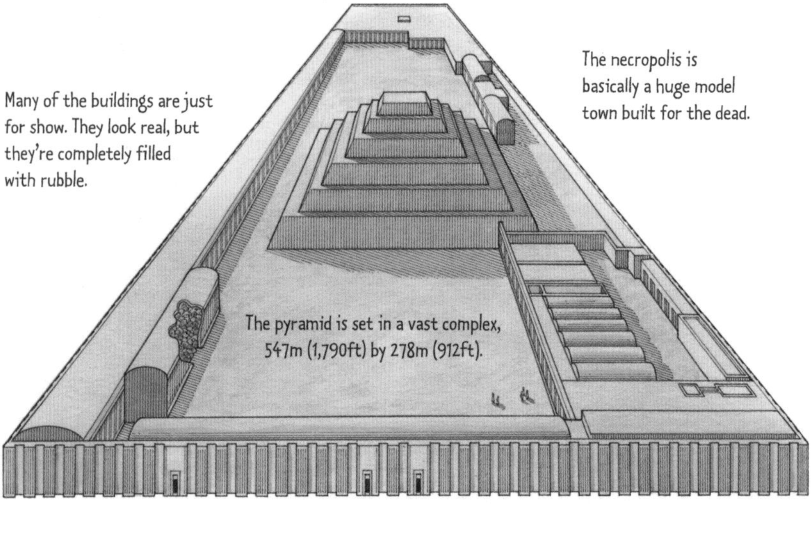

Stairway to heaven

This pyramid at Sakkara dates back about 1,500 years before your visit. It was built for the pharaoh, King Djoser, by placing six flat buildings (called *mastabas*), on top of one another, each one smaller than the one below. This formed a pyramid-like shape made out of steps.

The first pharaohs were just buried in *mastabas*, but the idea was that Djoser's spirit would be able to use the step pyramid as his very own stairway to heaven, to climb from his tomb, right up to the sky.

I think getting to heaven from one of the later, pointed pyramids involves climbing sunbeams... unless I misheard that.

The pyramid story

Mastaba

The earliest burial places were very simple.

Step pyramid

These are made from stacked *mastabas.*

True pyramid

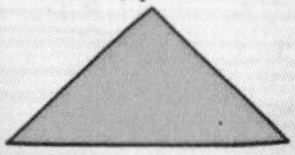

The latest design is smooth-sided.

A risky business

Tempting though the steps may be, I strongly warn against climbing them. I tried. Not only did the stone start to crumble under my scrambling fingers, I also got nabbed by the guards. It took a hefty bribe to make the threat of a lashing go away. As a rule, using a sacred tomb as a climbing wall is not a good idea.

Only the pharaoh's spirit is allowed up here.

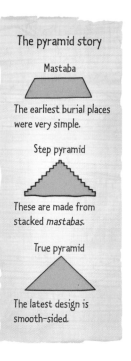

The cannibal pharaoh

King Unas ruled from around 2375 BC to 2345 BC. As a pharaoh, he was the earthly embodiment of a god.

But, that didn't seem enough for him. In the spells carved in his tomb, he threatens to gobble up all the other gods and absorb their wisdom.

Pyramid spells

For a truly spooky experience, you can climb down into the tomb of a pharaoh called Unas. It's actually very pretty, with a ceiling painted to look like a starry night sky. Carved all around are sacred messages and spells to help the dead pharaoh climb to his place in heaven. His tomb is under a pointed pyramid - the preferred route to heaven by Unas' time.

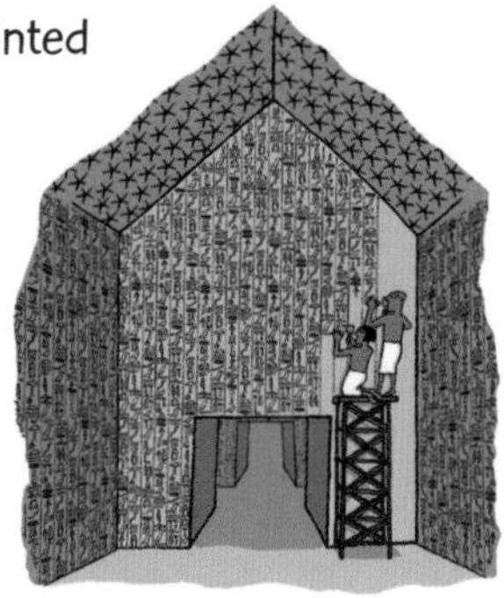

The scribes who carved the spells must have had sore arms when they'd finished.

"Unas eats their magic, swallows their spirits. The big ones are for his breakfast; the middle ones are for his dinner; the little ones are for his evening snack."

A pyramid text called the *Cannibal Hymn*

Noble young upstart

In the old days, the carved wall spells (called Pyramid Texts) were strictly for pharaohs. But years later, an ambitious young noble said: "I think I'll have a bit of that," and carved some of the spells in his own tomb. The idea caught on, and now even a rich peasant can buy a spell book, called the *Book of the Dead*, to put in a good word for him after he dies.

Part three:

Thebes: temples and tombs

Next stop, Thebes, where you'll see some amazing temples and tombs. You can even watch a mummy being made - an unsettling experience, but fascinating to watch.

It takes days to sail from Thebes from Memphis, so lie back, relax and enjoy the view. You could even brush up your Ancient Egyptian by chatting to the other passengers. (See pages 114-115 for tips.)

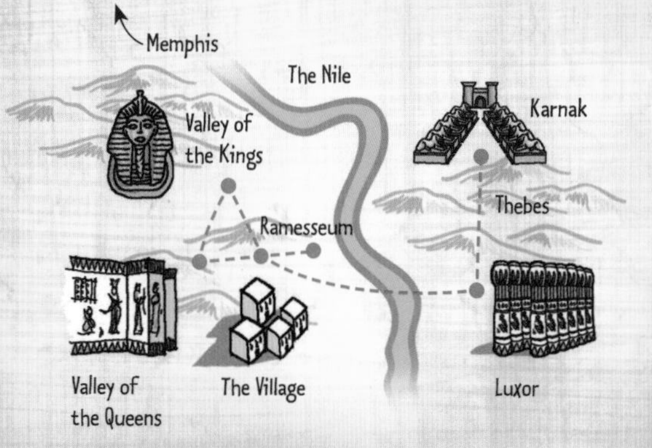

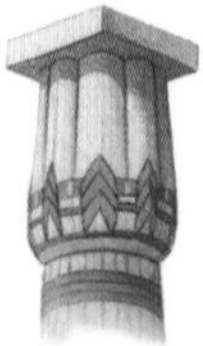

Papyrus bud style column

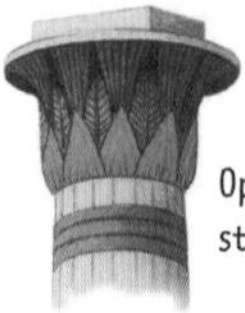

Open papyrus style column

Temple columns are often topped with plant-themed decorations. (These are meant to look like papyrus reeds.)

KEEP OUT!

In theory, the only person allowed to go inside temples to make offerings to the gods is the pharaoh.

But, despite being a god in human form, he's not able to be in several places at once, so he often delegates this job to local priests.

City of temples

The sights around Thebes are fairly spread out, so it's worth renting a house to use as a base, then hiring a donkey so you can get around without quite as much sweat.

The city of Thebes was the capital of Egypt for a while, but that doesn't make it all that special - the Ancient Egyptians change their capital on the whim of whoever's pharaoh.

What makes Thebes really stand out are all the splendid tombs and beautifully-decorated temples located close by.

WARNING!

The painted walls of temples are very impressive on the outside, but you can't just wander in and nose around. It's forbidden to enter most parts of most temples unless you're a priest or a pharaoh.

(I probably should've warned you about this earlier. Fingers crossed you read the whole book before visiting any temples.)

You can visit the outer courtyard, but wash yourself all over multiple times before you go in. (See page 107 for more on temple etiquette.)

A god's private house

Bear in mind that temples aren't places to go and pray. When you visit one, you're barging into the private residence of a god.

If you're lucky, you might even catch a glimpse of him (or her). Peer through the door and the dark halls of pillars. Can you see a golden statue? That's the god right there. (The god's spirit lives in the statue.)

Priests must feed, wash, and even entertain this statue. If they're not attentive enough, the god might get angry and send a plague or some other unpleasantness.

KEY

1. Obelisk (pointy column)
2. Pylon (entrance gate)
3. Courtyard (you can go in here)
4. Hypostyle hall (a dark hallway full of pillars)
5. Shrine (where a statue of the god is kept)
6. School, workshops and store rooms
7. Sacred pool where priests purify their bodies (a fancy way of saying 'have a wash').

A view of a typical temple. I've cut away the roof so you can see in – including the parts you can't visit.

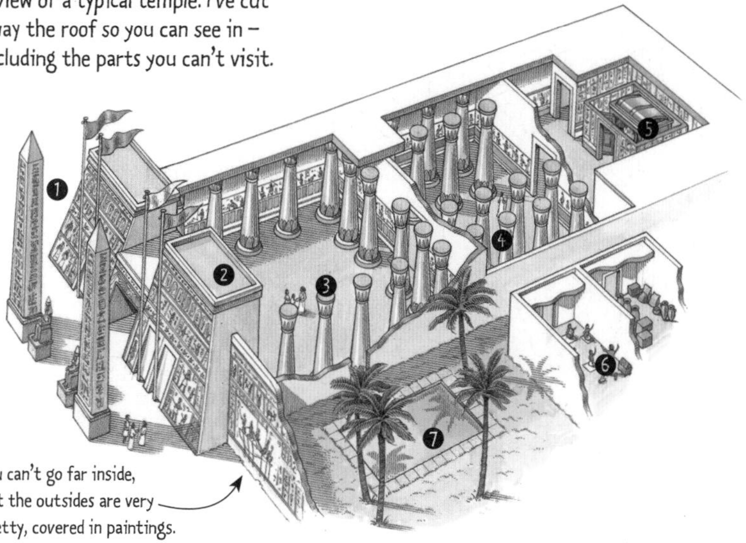

You can't go far inside, but the outsides are very pretty, covered in paintings.

The ram-headed sphinx is a symbol of the god Amun. (One part of Amun-Re)

Karnak: temple of Amun-Re

One must-see is the vast temple of Amun-Re, the most important local god. It's the largest building in the sprawl of temples known as Karnak. It was begun ages ago, but Ramesses II has added an extra *pylon* (gate) plus a *hypostyle* hall (hall with lots of pillars) at the front, as if to say, "Thousands of people might have spent centuries building this... but forget them. This is all about me. Me, me, me."

Locals claim it's where the world actually began. While plenty of priests think *their* local god created the world, Amun-Re's lot say he made the gods, too - even himself. If you're sceptical about this, keep quiet; a foreigner who insults the gods might not have a pleasant trip (or a particularly long life).

The leopardskin that this priest is wearing shows he's the top priest. Don't let him spot you nosing around.

A sneaky glimpse through the entrance will reveal the amazing, painted and carved pillars inside.

Luxor temple

Two miles south of Karnak, you'll find a smaller temple, originally built in 1380BC. Ramesses is adding a *pylon*, a courtyard, and, just in case anyone forgets who's boss around here, huge statues of himself.

The temple is dedicated to Amun-Re, his vulture goddess wife, Mut, and their moon god son, Khonsu. (And I thought my family was weird.) Although it's in the sweltering summer, it's worth timing your visit so you catch the spectacular festival of Opet (see page 110 for more details if you think you can handle the heat).

> **Top tips for tourists**
>
> Nº 16: Walls have ears
>
> Although you can't enter a god's sanctuary, many temples have a 'hearing ear' chapel round the back, or just a pair of ears carved on the wall, where anyone can pray.
>
> It's also where you can leave a *stela* (see page 39), to remind the gods to hear your prayers.

The Temple of Luxor

This avenue of sphinxes is two miles long, leading all the way to Karnak.

At Opet, priests carry Amun-Re's statue to Karnak in a small, boat-shaped shrine, along this avenue.

In the future (but still in Ancient Egypt), King Nectanebo I will 'improve' these statues of Amun by giving each one his own head.

NEXT STOP: VALLEY OF THE KINGS
(Tomb robbers, this way!)

Valley of the Kings

“I, together with other thieves … have continued to this day … robbing the tombs of the nobles and the people of the land who rest in the west of Thebes.”

A tomb robber on trial

If you cross the river, you'll find yourself in the Valley of the Kings - a burial site for pharaohs, where Ramesses II is planning to spend his eternal life.

As you approach the valley, you'll see what looks like a pyramid ahead, but it's really a mountain; the tombs are dug into tunnels far beneath.

Pyramids went out of fashion years ago; they kept getting robbed, leaving the pharaohs dead poor in the afterlife.

Top secret tombs are all the rage instead. Even if a robber finds one, he still has to face a snake goddess who lives down there, sending snakes and scorpions to attack anyone who disturbs her. "*Sssstop, thief!*"

Meretseger, the snake goddess, guardian of the tombs

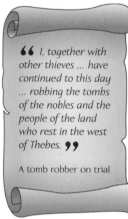

Tomb builders hard at work

Tomb workers are divided into two gangs of about forty (with plenty of friendly rivalry).

Overseers check that the tomb measurements match the architect's plans.

The tomb builders

A royal tomb takes years to build. It has to be fit for a king, after all.

Royal corpses-to-be like to get involved in planning their tombs, and each ruler starts preparing merrily for his own death as soon as his bottom hits the throne. If you're going to spend eternity somewhere, you'd better like the way it's decorated, after all.

You can go and watch the workers building Ramesses II's underground dream home, but it's a hot and dusty business, so take plenty of water. The tunnels can be cramped, too, so don't get in the way - unless you want a pile of rubble to land on your foot.

You'll see all sorts, from the foremen checking that the walls are straight and porters lugging rubble to painters expertly plying their trade. Even the half-finished paintings can be breathtaking.

Top tips for tourists

№ 17: Stop thief!

Helping yourself to a little tomb souvenir may be tempting, but best avoided, as the punishments are severe. For example, many tomb robbers are skewered on a stake like a kebab.

Tombs are lit by linen wicks burning in saucers of oil.

The rubble is carried away in baskets, often by the workmen's sons.

A cut above

You may think that tomb workers are slaves, but they're highly-skilled craftsmen with a better life than most.

They work hard, but they're paid richly, and have enough time off to enjoy doodling on shards of broken pots.

At death, they'll have every Egyptian's dream: a tip-top tomb of their own.

The Village

If you want to explore the Valley of the Kings for a few days, you've got a choice between camping or staying in the 'Place of Truth', often called 'the Village' (Deir el-Medina to modern Egyptians). It's a purpose-built, walled village for the tomb workers, near the Valley of the Kings.

Sadly, there are no flashy mod cons, or even incredibly basic ancient cons, if you rent a house here. It's bound to be a) dark b) stuffy and c) smell like dung (animals live inside). Windows are just slits, too. On the whole, it would be better to stay elsewhere and just have a quick look around.

A worker's house opened up for a peek inside (dung not pictured)

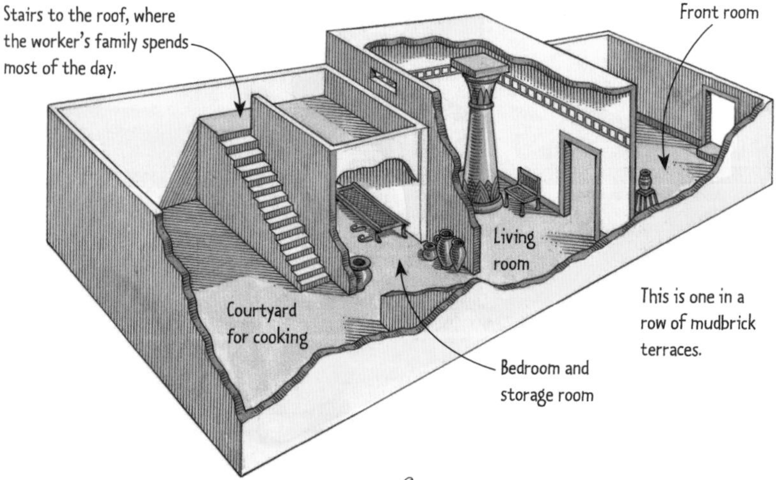

The Boy King

One tomb you *won't* be visiting belongs to Tutankhamun, who died about 100 years before your trip - it's sealed and very heavily guarded.

But if you tell anyone you've been to Ancient Egypt (and they don't think you're barking mad) they're bound to ask about King Tut, as he's a big celeb in our time.

You'll have to disappoint them, as Tut didn't do anything special as king, and died before his 20th birthday. He's only famous because his grave wasn't robbed as often as the other kings' (only twice) so he left behind some fabulous bling.

Tut's treasures

This wooden model, covered in gold, shows young Tut on a raft, about to hurl his harpoon at something.

Part of a couch in the shape of a cow goddess, left in Tutankhamun's tomb for him to rest on when he's sleepy.

Here's one of King Tut's magnificent coffins. You might be able to see this or other Tut treasures when you get home. This coffin can be seen in modern Cairo.

Valley of the Queens

The Valley of the Queens is the burial site for the pharaoh's wives and children. If you visit before his wife Nefertari's death, you can see her amazing tomb being built.

After her death, Ramesses still has hundreds of wives to comfort him, but a visit to Nef's tomb will show you he loved her most of all. (Almost as much as he loves himself.) Getting in is tricky, with the *Medjay* prowling around, but I say risk it.*

Starry eyed

If you walk into the burial chamber, or 'golden hall', of Nefertari's tomb (see picture below) you'd be struck by the ceiling. Ouch! Only joking, it's not that low, and all I meant to say before I was distracted by an awful joke was that the ceiling is stunning. It's a deep blue, decorated with golden stars.

These stand for the spirits of the dead who the queen will spend her afterlife with.

A sneaky peek inside Nefertari's tomb

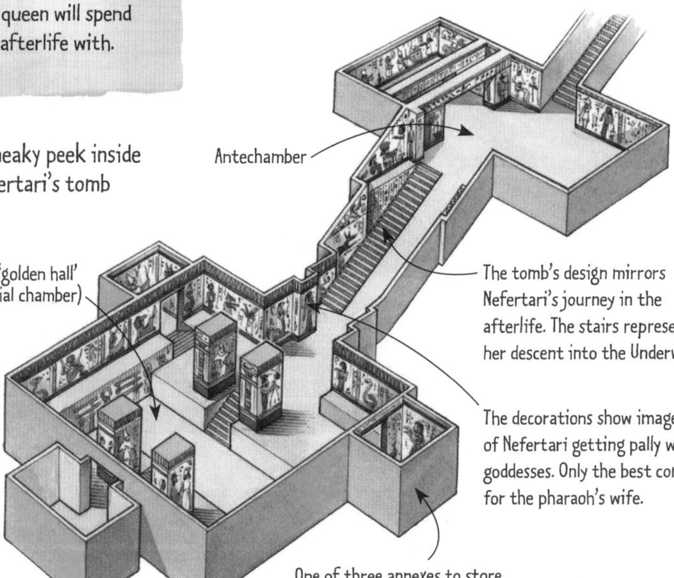
Antechamber
The 'golden hall' (burial chamber)
The tomb's design mirrors Nefertari's journey in the afterlife. The stairs represent her descent into the Underworld.
The decorations show images of Nefertari getting pally with goddesses. Only the best company for the pharaoh's wife.
One of three annexes to store treasure (for a while, anyway)

Picturing the afterlife

A visit to the queen's tomb is risky, as I said, but rewarding - both for you *and* the guards you'll have to bribe. Your reward? The chance to see some truly magical pictures; they're literally magical, according to the Egyptians.

Look at the images on the walls. You might see detailed pictures of food, clothing, jewels, pets or servants. All these are supposed to come to life in the next world. So, as you peer at a scene of a feast, you're seeing a sneak menu preview of what the queen will enjoy in heaven when she dies.

This servant isn't performing a balancing act: it's the artist's way of showing us not just his fancy box, but the goodies inside it, too.

The Ramesseum

North-east of the Valley of the Queens, you can visit the mortuary temples (that is, places where pharaohs are worshipped after they die).

Depending on which year you visit, you should be able to see Ramesses's temple being built. If you visit before it's finished, people shouldn't be too fussy about you going in, as it's not as holy at that point. You might even see the shrine where part of the pharaoh's spirit will live after death; almost like nosing around his bedroom!

Ramesses's temple isn't short of – surprise, surprise – giant statues of Ramesses.

*NOTE: My lawyer told me to add: "By buying this book, readers agree all risks they take are their own. Especially if they're rude, or don't bathe enough to meet Egyptian standards."

Perfect people

People in Egyptian tomb art may look strange to you. Chests are shown front on, yet faces and limbs are in profile.

People don't really stand like that, but Egyptian tomb artists are less interested in being realistic and more interested in showing off the most recognizable parts of a person, from a handsome profile to broad, manly shoulders.

The idea is to show the deceased as a *Ka*, or a perfect immortal self.

Decorators for the dead

If you visit a nearly-finished tomb or mortuary temple, you can witness the highly skilled teams of tomb painters at work. It's a fiddly process, and the artists have super-strict rules to follow. For example, all human figures have to be drawn with their features spaced out in a particular way.

If the painters don't make everything look perfect, it could ruin the pharaoh's afterlife. These are 'magical' images, supposed to bring success and comfort in the world to come.

The first sketches are done using a grid which is erased later.
Painting the first sketch
Mixing paint
Checking the plan

Sticky-out pictures

Before the last details are painted, carvers chip around the outlines so that they stand out. (This is called 'relief'.)

As the artists carefully add the final layers of paint - all home-made, as there are no art shops in Egypt - check which paints they're using. Different shades of paint have symbolic meanings. For example, red stands for chaos *or* power and black stands for death *or* fertility. (Yes, it is confusing.)

"I am an artisan excellent at my craft. I know how to make pigments ... without letting the fire burn them ... None will know this but me and my eldest son."

Irtysen the artisan, keeping it in the family

You will find the odd gesture towards realism – since men work outside more than women, their skin is shown as tanned.
Foreman (He's in charge.)
This sculptor is carving a raised relief, cutting away the background so that the figure stands out.
The lamp oil is mixed with salt so the wicks don't smoke and spoil the painting.

> **Top tips for tourists**
>
> № 18: An iron stomach
>
> Most people pale at the sight of someone's brains being tugged out through their nostrils*. So be wise: never visit an embalmer's workshop too close to lunch.
>
> *See page 68

Mummy factories

If you have a strong enough stomach you can visit an embalmer's workshop, where mummies are made. You'll find these in the City of the Dead, which is west of the river.

Egyptians are highly skilled at embalming (preserving) bodies. Just *how* they do it is top secret, but if you give enough copper weights to a poor-looking apprentice embalmer, I bet he'd give you the full tour.

Try to avoid bumping into his boss, though. (He's easy to spot. He's the one in the scary jackal mask, which represents Anubis, the god of embalming.)

Embalmers at work

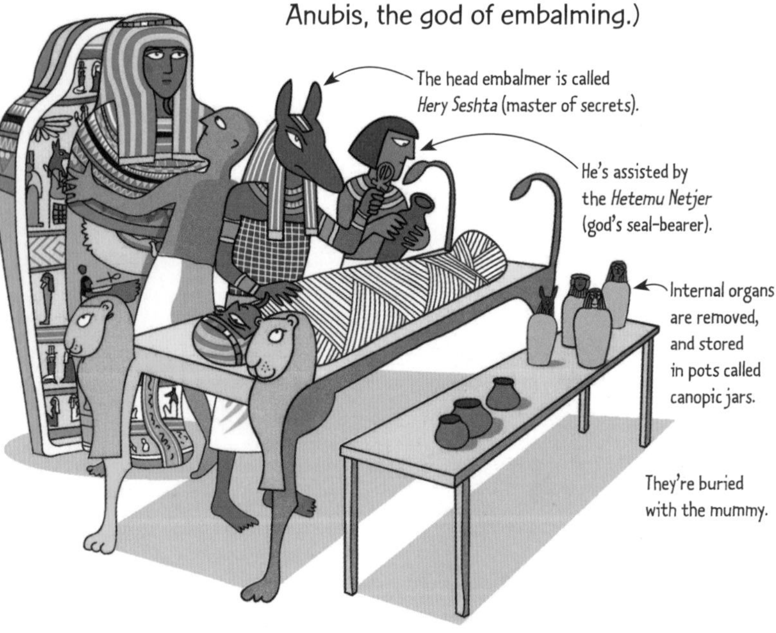

The head embalmer is called *Hery Seshta* (master of secrets).
He's assisted by the *Hetemu Netjer* (god's seal-bearer).
Internal organs are removed, and stored in pots called canopic jars.
They're buried with the mummy.

How mummies work

Watching a body have its insides scooped out will be a memorable experience to say the least. (I still remember my visit... often... at night... when I'm all alone...)

But, before you see this gory ritual for yourself, I'll let you in on a few mummy facts - they should help you understand what you're seeing.

For starters, how do mummies work? 'By magic' is the short answer. Apparently, each mummy, or *sah*, acts as a sort of magical anchor for the dead person's *ka* (soul), allowing them to eat, drink and party forever in the afterlife.

Canopic jars

Canopic jars depict four gods, the sons of Horus, who protect the organs inside. Baboon-headed Hapy looks after lungs; Kebehsenuef the falcon attends intestines; the jackal Duamutef guards the stomach; Imsety is on liver duty.

Magic bandages

One of the 'active ingredients' in mummy magic are the bandages that are wrapped around the corpse. After the body's been prepared (more on that in a minute), linen strips, treated with special oils, are applied. This transforms a corpse into the body of Osiris himself. (I don't really understand how that happens to be honest. While my Ancient Egyptian's good, it's not good enough to make sense of the trickier magical stuff.)

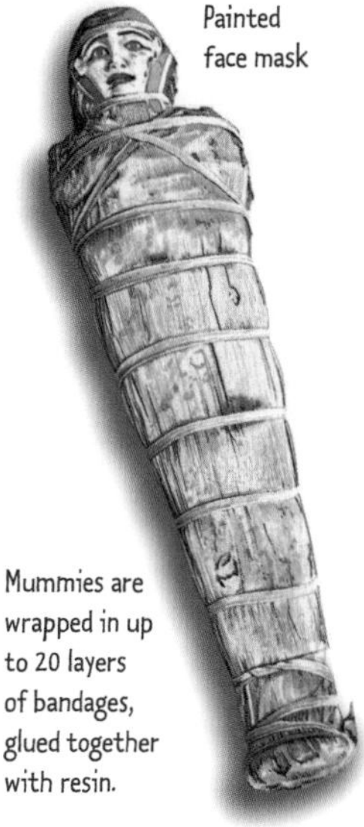

Mummies are wrapped in up to 20 layers of bandages, glued together with resin.

Mummification at a glance

After the body's cut open, the organs are removed and stored.

The body is then dried out in natron crystals.

A priest casts spells on amulets (charms) that will protect the mummy.

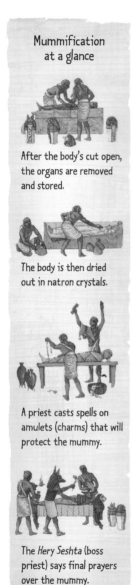

The *Hery Seshta* (boss priest) says final prayers over the mummy.

Mysteries of mummy-making

When you visit the embalmers, ask if the current client's 'treatment' cost a packet - or peanuts. As you might expect, it's more fun to watch the priciest ones, though cheap ones might be easier to crash.

Hard-up corpses (or those whose families don't like them much) are gutted and rinsed with Nile water and palm wine, then dried in *natron* (a type of salt) for 40 days - in fact, the whole thing takes 70 days, so ask for a tour when they're at an interesting bit.

Thinking with your heart

The *really* cool stuff's just for royals and nobles who can afford to pay through the nose. Speaking of... the first step in the deluxe service is to scrape out the brain through the nostrils with a hook. (Egyptians think the brain's pretty useless, you see.)

The *Hery Sheshta* slits open the body, while everyone throws stones at him for defiling the dead (not too hard: he is the boss!). The organs are then embalmed, and most go in jars: but the heart is put back, as Ancient Egyptians believe it's the organ you think with, so it's extra-important.

It's a wrap

After the forty-day drying process, the body's stuffed (to improve its shape), perfumed with myrrh (which also helps preserve it), then softened with oils.

Finally, the bandages are applied, with lots of charms stuffed between the layers - like presents in a gruesome pass the parcel. These are to protect the mummy.

As the *Hery Heb* (another priest) reads spells over the body, the boss priest ties the final, magical bandages. The last touch is a mask, and the mummy, or *sah*, is ready.

> *"My corpse is permanent, it will not perish nor be destroyed in this land for ever."*
>
> Spell 154, from the *Book of the Dead*

Animummies

It's not just people who get all this pampering after death. Sacred animals, from bulls to cats and dogs get mummified and buried in serious style. The rich even give their pets the mummy treatment sometimes.

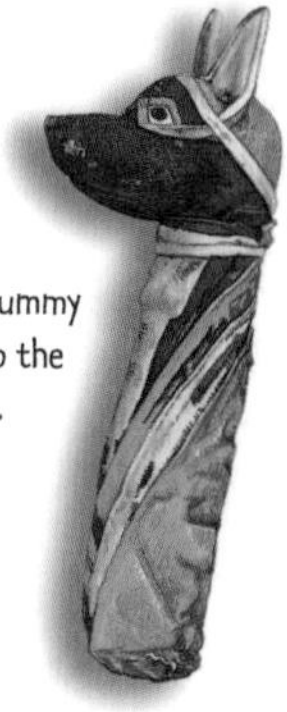

This dog mummy is sacred to the god Anubis.

A funeral procession for an Apis bull (see page 48).

First class travel

Coffins are painted with decorative scenes and magical signs to help the deceased through the trials of the afterlife.

Very rich people or royals don't just have one wooden coffin. They get a whole nest of coffins, with a gold or a gold-plated inner coffin plus a sarcophagus (stone coffin) to put it all in.

What next, mummy?

You can never be too careful in the afterlife, so each completed mummy is put into a coffin (or sometimes several, see left).

This is human-shaped and brightly painted but, as with tomb paintings, these pictures aren't just meant to look pretty. They offer even more magical protection and help for the departing soul. They'll certainly need it as they voyage through the dark nights of *Duat* - the Egyptian underworld. (Ask an embalmer what each picture means.)

Here's how a mummy is magically protected inside a human-shaped coffin.

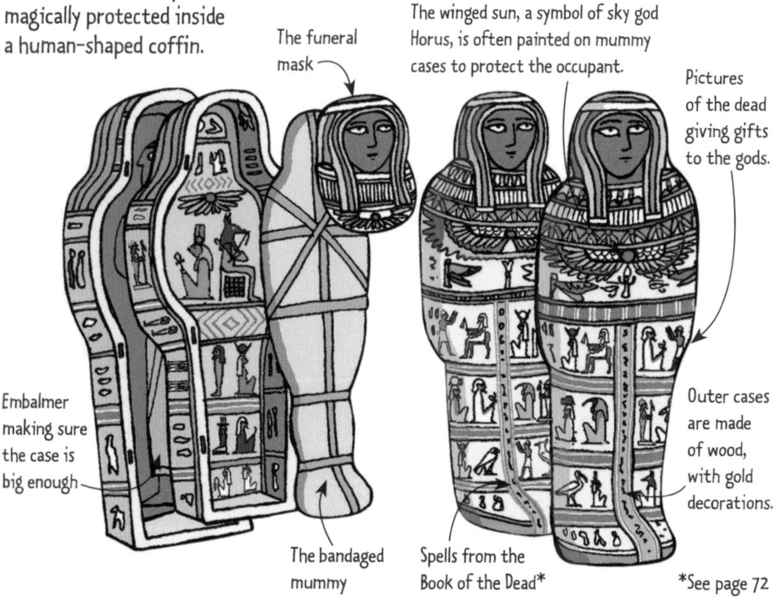
The funeral mask
The winged sun, a symbol of sky god Horus, is often painted on mummy cases to protect the occupant.
Pictures of the dead giving gifts to the gods.
Embalmer making sure the case is big enough
Outer cases are made of wood, with gold decorations.
The bandaged mummy
Spells from the Book of the Dead*

*See page 72

Coffin couture

As with clothes, there are fashions in coffins, too. Egyptians will shop for their own, long before they need one. Why not pretend you're a customer and ask to see the latest models? (Hint: black coffins are so over. Yellow coffins with blue and red decorations are the only thing to be seen dead in.)

Customers who go for out-of-date coffin styles can save a packet.

In high spirits

Egyptians believe that each person has several spirits. If you hear people at the embalmers talking about a mummy's *Ka*, or its *Ba*, or its *Akh*, this is what they mean...

Ka: the life force, or 'double' (the self you are in dreams). It can move around the tomb, so doors are painted on coffins to let it out. The *Ka*'s symbol is a pair of raised arms, so look out for those on coffins.

Ba: a bird-like spirit that roams the Earth by day, or sails the skies in the Sun-god's boat, but returns to the tomb at night.

Akh: symbolized by an ibis, this spirit's born at death, and rises up to live with the stars.

One type of spirit, the *Ba*, is symbolized by a bird with the head of the deceased.

Coffins have clear (if flattering) portraits of their residents, so the wandering *Ba* can find its way to its own body again.

The Book of the Dead

“O Apep, you enemy of Re. Get back you fiend, before his piercing beams! Re has defeated your words ... The Lynx has torn out your heart, the Scorpion has bound you in chains ...”

Spell 39 from the *Book of the Dead*, to defeat the evil serpent Apep

Egyptians don't have the expression 'better safe than sorry', but they certainly seem to live, or at least die, by it.

As well as magic coffins and mummy charms, each dead person gets extra spells to get through the underworld safely. These used to be carved inside tombs, but nowadays, a page of spells is slipped into the coffin. You can buy one as a souvenir (and if the worst happens... you'll be ready).

Top tips for tourists

№ 19: Good spelling

If you buy a Book of the Dead, check it has the essentials. Spell 23 lets your soul talk: vital for self-defence (and being invited to parties).

Spell 51 means you won't have to walk upside-down for eternity, for example. Or for some after-death relaxation, Spell 17 even lets you enjoy a nice board game.

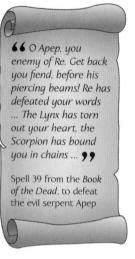

“Oh, and I'll need a spell to stop my robes getting dirty in the afterlife.”

In the future, this pamphlet will be known as the *Book of the Dead*, but Egyptians call it *Spells for Coming Forth by Day*. (They're not very into short, snappy titles.) The rich have theirs customized, picking their own spells; poorer customers buy standard copies with a gap for their name.

Keep your heart light

If you buy a *Book of the Dead,* you might find it confusing, as there aren't any words as such - Ancient Egyptians use a kind of picture writing known as hieroglyphics. (See pages 115-118 for a crash course.)

But, the main thing you need to know to understand the book - and to know what's in store one day if the Egyptians are right - is that a dead person is put on trial by the gods. His or her heart's weighed against a 'feather of truth'. If the heart's heavier, it's bad news - the soul is doomed forever.

Scarab beetles like the one on this jewel are thought to protect the mummy's heart.

A scene from the Book of the Dead, showing the weighing of the heart.

Gods make up the jury.

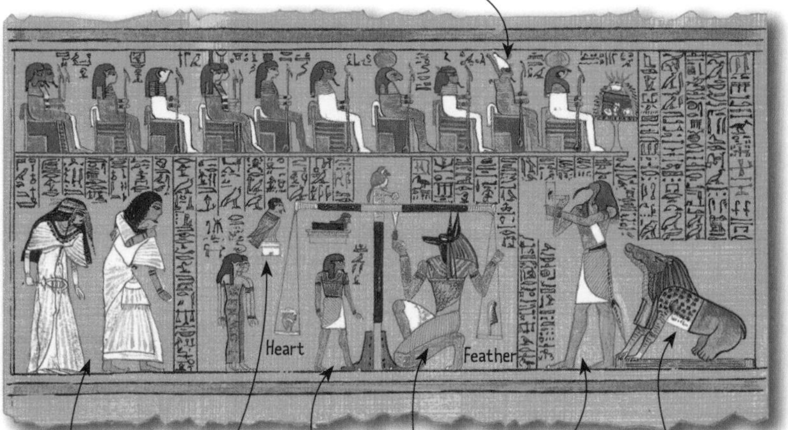

The dead man, and his wife.

His *Ba* perches above goddesses of fortune and rebirth.

God of destiny

Anubis weighs the heart.

Thoth records the outcome.

Ammit, a monster, gobbles the heart if it fails the test.

A funeral procession

> *❝ Think of the day of your burial ... how a funeral procession shall be made for you on the day you rejoin the earth ... a case of gold, a mask of lapis lazuli, the heavens above you, placed in the bier. The oxen drawing you, the musicians before you, the Mu-u dancers dancing at the door of your tomb.* ❞
>
> From *The Tale of Sinuhe*

But, before facing judgement, a mummy has to be buried. And, as a tourist, an Egyptian funeral is a must-see sight.

Luckily (for you at least) you're bound to catch one while visiting tomb-packed Thebes. Death rates are high and many Egyptians don't survive childhood. Even the rich, with their cushy lives, rarely make it to sixty.

You may even see a royal funeral, as Ramesses has hundreds of wives and children - odds are that time will be up for at least one of them during your trip.

The long walk to the tomb

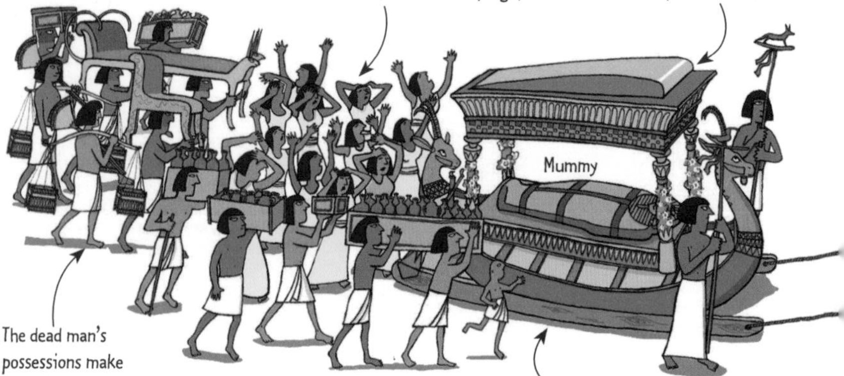
Professional mourners follow the funeral barge. (Tourist tip: look sad, but wear earplugs.)
The mummy will lie on this gold-plated bier (coffin stand).
Mummy
The dead man's possessions make it look as if he's moving house (which he is, in a way).
The barge symbolizes the soul's voyage to the Underworld.

The final journey

What can you expect to see at an Egyptian funeral? Well, you'll hear it long before you see it, with the mourners' shrill wailing rising above the priests' solemn drone.

But soon, if it's someone important being buried, you'll catch a glimpse of the golden bier (coffin stand).

Streams of servants will be following it, laden with everything a well-heeled mummy could need in the afterlife: from furniture to chests of clothes and food.

If you hear a loud, screechy "Mee ee Mu-u!" sound, don't be scared. It's just the accompaniment for the *Mu-u* dancers, who perform a strange, high-stepping dance and bless the mummy on its final journey. If you can't spot them by the crazy dancing, look out for men in tall reed hats.

A *Sem* (funeral priest) wearing a leopard skin heads the procession, burning incense.

Once the funeral barge has crossed the Nile, oxen drag it on a sled to the tomb.

Top tips for tourists

№ 20: See how the other half dies

For the poor, buried in the sand with little more than a few pots, the afterlife looks no rosier than this life.

Some are buried near rich tombs, hoping that their *Ka* may catch a few scraps from the offerings left for the noble dead.

Funeral masks

Mummy masks vary in price. The cheapest are made of a sort of papier mâché, while posh ones are gilded. Only royalty and other big shots can afford solid gold, like this gleaming mask, made for a pharaoh.

NEXT STOP NUBIA
(Take some water!)

Magical tools with symbolic meaning are used to awaken the mummy's senses.

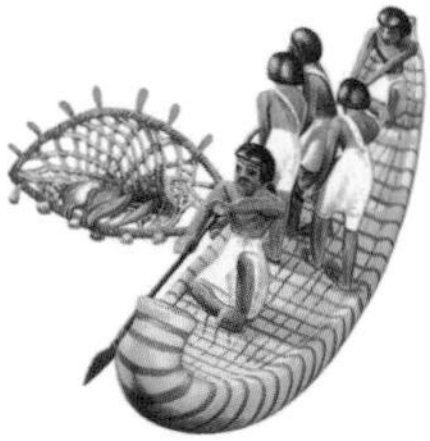

A model boat left in a tomb should ensure the peckish *Ka* has a good supply of fresh fish.

Some *shabtis* will fit into your pocket.

Open wide

When the funeral procession reaches the tomb where the body's going to be buried, priests will carefully carry the mummy into the spooky darkness of the tomb.

You won't be able to go inside, but you'll hear them chanting, "*Waab! Waab!*" This is part of a ritual known as the *Opening of the Mouth* - a spell to allow the dead man's *Ka* to breathe, talk, eat and enjoy his new home.

For the relatives, this isn't really goodbye. They'll be back on festival days to bring the *Ka* food and drink - in return, they'll expect protection from bad luck. (Even when you're dead, there's no such thing as a free lunch.)

Mini-mummies

Egyptians think the next life is a lot like this one, so crops still have to be sown, and canals dug. That means someone's got to sow and dig even after death.

Unsurprisingly, eternal drudgery doesn't appeal, so everyone's buried with magical mummy models called *shabtis*, that turn into willing slaves. You could buy one of these as a souvenir - though I'm sorry to say it won't do your chores for you while you're alive.

Part four:
Nubia

If you're feeling very adventurous, you could sail south of Egypt's border into Nubia, plunging into the ancient heart of Africa.

The desert closes in on either side, and everything is much quieter, as most creatures don't thrive in places this hot and dry. (Including you, so stay in the shade.) Often, all you'll hear is the flapping of the sail. But press on! There are some wonderful sights in the Nubian desert.

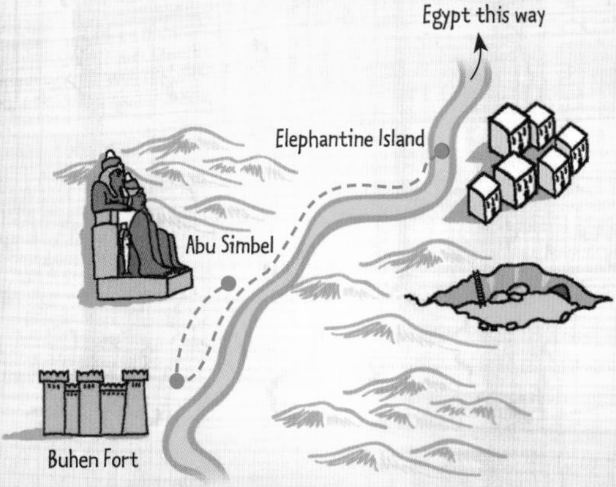

An expedition to Nubia

To get to Nubia, just continue south along the Nile. The country begins at the '1st Cataract' - one of a series rocky blockages in the Nile that boats can't get past. (You might have to help carry the boat for a bit.)

Nubia is ruled by the Egyptians, so if you just behave as you would in Egypt (plenty of washing, plenty of bribery) you should fit right in. But beware of the Sun; it gets so fierce here that the sky turns yellow. Cover up and stay in the shade when you can.

War & peace

The history of Egypt and Nubia is a troubled one – especially for the Nubians. Egypt rules them and is always nabbing lots of their lovely gold and ivory (from elephant tusks), as 'tribute'.

But, still, it's usually fairly peaceful. With Egyptian towns and temples springing up all over the place, Nubians are taking to the new way of life like crocs to water.

Nubians are skilled archers. In fact, Egyptians sometimes call Nubia the 'Land of the Bow'.

A map of Egypt and Nubia

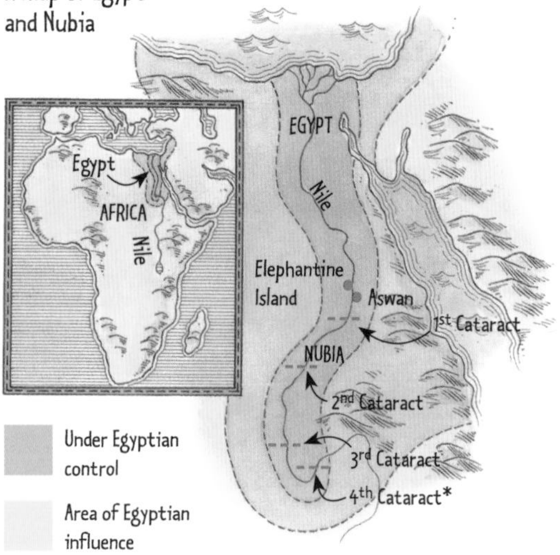

*Nubia lies between the 1st Cataract and the 2nd Cataract, but Egypt rules all the way up to the 4th Cataract.

The island of elephants past

On the way to Nubia, you could stop off at Elephantine Island, by the city of Aswan. Sorry to disappoint, but it's not full of elephants. It got its name because they used to trade elephants' ivory tusks there.

The reason it's worth a visit is because a) it's a handy place to stock up on supplies for the journey ahead and b) it's a great place for souvenir shopping.

All the riches of Africa pass through here, and some of the best incense and trinkets don't make it any further. So, haggle hard and you could bag some excellent bargains.

> *"Here gold is found in great abundance and huge elephants, and ebony, and all sorts of trees growing wild."*
>
> Herodotus on Nubia

An ancient ivory game piece

The Nilometer

On the island's southeastern shore you'll see a narrow staircase stepping down into the river. This simple yet nifty device is called the Nilometer, used to measure the height of the annual flood. This means officials can decide whether it will be a good or bad year for crops, and set taxes to match. (The wetter it is, the better the harvest... and the higher the taxes. You win some, you lose some.)

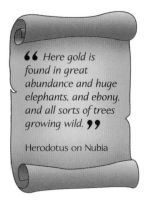

High tide means high taxes. Though, on the plus side, it means better harvests, too.

Deep in the desert

The mines that yield the most gold are buried deep in the Eastern Desert.

The days there are unendurably hot, and the nights bitterly cold. Only the most vicious criminals are sent here, and you have to travel there with armed guards. I'd give it a miss if I were you.

Gold mines

As you sail through Nubia, stop off at the gold mines to see why the Egyptians call this place the 'Land of Gold'. (Among other names, since, 'Why use one name when four will do?' seems to be their motto.)

The gold that's dug up here might be pretty, but the way it's mined isn't. The miners are criminals and prisoners of war, forced to crawl into deep, hot, narrow tunnels to hack out heavy lumps of rock. I imagine they're seriously regretting their crimes (or losing that battle) by now.

You can watch gold being unearthed at a Nubian mine.

Heating crushed rock to extract the gold
Soldiers run and guard the camp.
Not all the mining is done underground. Here are some miners working at an open rockface.

Sacred metal

Thanks to all this hard work - not that the miners get any thanks - Nubia's mines supply Egypt with enough gold to make foreign kings green with envy.

But in Egypt, gold is more than just treasure. It's a symbol of eternity, and gods are actually supposed to have gold skin and bones. So when you're visiting a temple, look out for golden paintings or statues. They're almost certainly gods or gods-in-human-form a.k.a. pharaohs.

If you see a golden statue of a cow, you're not on a very posh farm – it will be an image of a cow goddess.

Raining gold

If you meet any government types on your travels - or sail with them through Nubia (see right) - ask to tag along next time they visit the 'Window of Appearances' at one of the pharaoh's palaces. These are balconies where the pharaoh stands to toss down gold collars to loyal officials.

It's a strange sight - I can't picture the prime minister where I come from chucking gold at a politician who's done a good job. But when you're in Ancient Egypt, you'll come to expect strangeness everywhere you go.

Top tips for tourists

№ 21: Split the cost

Unfortunately, getting to Nubia isn't cheap. But if money's tight, you could sign up as a deckhand with some traders. Or you could ask around to see if a minor official will go halves on renting a boat.

If you're lucky, he might get you into some fancy parties, too, where you'll get even more free stuff.

NEXT STOP BUHEN FORT
(No cheeking the guards...)

Egyptian forts

Scribes make a careful note of everything going in and out of the fort.

After you've been sailing for about eight days, you'll reach a chain of nine ancient forts that lie along the Nile.

They look bleak and forbidding, but if you manage to get inside, you'll find a whole town full of lively markets, rowdy taverns, bustling barracks and busy bakeries.

The storerooms are filled with treasures, ready to be shipped off around the known world: ebony (heavy dark wood) and ivory, amethysts and emeralds, ostrich feathers and panther skins. You can see why the place is heavily guarded. So... how can you get inside?

One of the great Nubian forts under attack by foolhardy raiders

Battlements protect the soldiers, while holes in the walls let archers rain arrows down on the enemy.

Buhen fort

The gigantic Buhen fort is the most impressive fort of all. The first time I visited it, I went alone. Big mistake - the guards turned me away as, unsurprisingly, nosy, idle foreigners aren't welcome.

But, on my way back up to Egypt, I tried again, this time with an group of traders - I still had enough pepper with me to persuade them to let me join their gang.

When you visit, you can either tag along with some merchants like I did, and pretend to be a trader, or you could join up with an official party of visiting government types - perhaps claiming to be a foreign ruler... and backing up your claim with many, many presents.

Mind you, if they suspect you're a raider or a spy, you might get a very in-depth tour of the gold mines instead of the fort.

A numbers game

Buhen fort was built to strike despair into the hearts of the rowdy local tribes.

It's a question of numbers. Would you fancy your chances against an enemy sitting smugly behind 8 million bricks arranged into walls 8m (26ft) high and 4m (13ft) thick?

It doesn't matter how good you are with a bow and arrow (and some of the raiders are very, very good), those walls are just too strong.

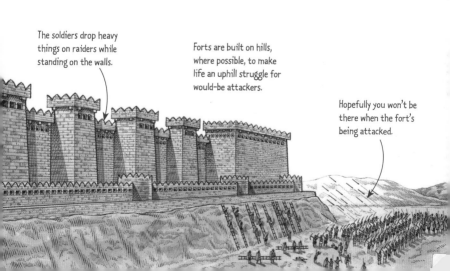

The soldiers drop heavy things on raiders while standing on the walls.

Forts are built on hills, where possible, to make life an uphill struggle for would-be attackers.

Hopefully you won't be there when the fort's being attacked.

War stories

If a soldier is grumpy, don't take it personally. He has a hard life.

If you're interested in how Ancient Egyptians fight, why not strike up a conversation with an off-duty soldier in a tavern, since you're in a fort already? (Talk to one *on*-duty and the only conversation you'll get will be, "Halt! Who goes there!")

If you meet a soldier who says he drives a chariot into battle, treat him with extra respect. Charioteers are the army's top dogs - they sometimes ride into battle right beside the pharaoh. They also tend to be loaded; horses and chariots are pricey, so learning to drive is a rich kid's hobby.

> *"He may not rest, and only has water every third day. His body is sick. The enemy surrounds him and he is told: "Forward, valiant soldier! Win a good name for yourself!" But he no longer knows what he's doing. His body is weak, his legs fail him."*
>
> A scribe's assessment of a soldier's life

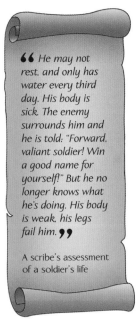

Ramesses, the richest charioteer of them all

For most soldiers, life in the army is tough. The discipline is harsh (and not always fair). But at least they get fed well, and the army doctors tend to be excellent.

Why bother fighting?

The Egyptians aren't very warlike these days, as they've already conquered plenty of people. Still, there's always someone who doesn't quite know they're beaten for the Egyptian army to fight.

Going away to fight has one big drawback (aside from the risk of getting stabbed) - if you die away from home, who'll prepare your body for the afterlife?

Free stuff? Forward march!

Ramesses lures young men into the army with high wages and gives free land and slaves to heroic fighters. But before you're tempted to sign up, bear in mind that recruits are toughened by forced marches, wrestling competitions and beatings. I'd stick to watching the soldiers on parade.

If you see an army division heading off to fight, you'll see all kinds of people tagging along, including doctors, priests and cooks.

NEXT STOP ABU SIMBEL
(Could be costly!)

Abu Simbel

The entrance leads into the heart of the mountain.

Before you leave Nubia, make sure you see the temple at Abu Simbel. It's incredibly grand, with four vast statues at the front entrance. The shadowy inside parts are built right into the mountain.

As you walk towards the temple, you'll see the huge stone statues of four men sitting on thrones. Actually, it's not four men; it's Ramesses II, four times over, and twenty times larger than life.

He towers over everything, reminding the Nubians that their faraway ruler is very mighty indeed - just in case they forget they've been conquered and start getting any silly ideas about ruling themselves. Basically, the temple's there to say: "Ramesses is awesome. You are puny. Behave!"

The smaller statue on the left is of Nefertari, Ramesses's chief wife.

The statues are painted to stand out against the mountainside.

Inside the temple

As with most temples, only the pharaoh and his priests are allowed inside. But, for the right bribe, the guards can experience a sudden lapse in concentration. They may even fall asleep. In any case, they certainly didn't notice any foreigners going this way, no, definitely not.

Once you're safely (if expensively) inside, it'll take a while for your eyes to adjust to the gloom. But the first thing you'll see are eight giant statues of Osiris (god of the dead, remember?) brooding above you.

The walls are covered in carvings of Ramesses's victories in battle. One shows him in his chariot at the battle of Kadesh, beating an entire army single-handed. (I'm sure that's *exactly* how it happened.)

Further into the temple, deep inside the rock, lies a sacred room housing four stone figures - Amun-Re, a king among gods, Re-Harakhte, a Sun god, Ramesses himself (who's a god too, remember), and Ptah, a god of the Underworld and darkness.

Twice a year, on 20th October and 20th February, something very special happens in this shadowy hall... (See right.)

Gaze at the statues of Osiris. Look familiar? They should do; each one has Ramesses's face.

Re's rays

Twice a year, for just five minutes at dawn, the Sun shines directly through the temple entrance. The rays of the Sun bathe three of the statues in light. Only Ptah is left in the dark. But, he's a god of darkness, so I doubt he minds much.

In the images you'll see of Nefertari, she'll be wearing a heavy-looking crown like this.

The temple of lurve

Beside the main temple you'll find a smaller one dedicated to Nefertari, one of Ramesses's wives, and Hathor, a goddess of all kinds of nice things, from love and beauty to music and cheerfulness.

When you visit, bear in mind that it's highly unusual for the wife of a pharaoh to get her own temple. The fact that Nefertari's temple has statues of her out at the front - and the fact that these are the same size as the statues of Ramesses - is even more amazing. As a love token, it's certainly more impressive than flowers or chocolates.

"My love is unique - no one can rival her, for she is the most beautiful woman alive. Just by passing, she has stolen away my heart."

A poem carved on the tomb of Nefertari by her husband, Ramesses II

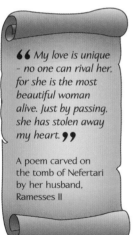

Usually, pharaohs make sure that their statues are bigger than anyone else's. But Ramesses made an exception for his beloved Nefertari.

Ramesses called Nefertari: 'the one for whom the Sun shines'. Maybe he's just a great big softy at heart? (Mind you, if he catches you in his wife's temple, he's unlikely to show that side of his personality.)

Part five:

Any other questions?

I think that's most of the important sights covered. But, as I near the end of this book, I realize there are lots of things I haven't told you yet about life in Ancient Egypt - where even the most everyday things can seem bizarre to modern eyes.

So, this section is an attempt to fill in the gaps and make sure you know everything you need to know to fit in and have fun - from how to write in Egyptian to how to snag an invite to a glitzy party.

Hungry? Bored? Egyptian parties will cure both.

Tips for shopping trips

Shopping is always tricky when you're on a trip abroad. There are all kinds of obstacles, from getting used to foreign coins to the language barrier. But in Ancient Egypt, there's another more basic problem: there aren't any shops.

Or at least, not the kind you're used to. But they do have plenty of markets and craft workshops where you can buy everything you need and, if you're anything like me, some silly tat you really *don't* need.

At a fish stall, make sure the local cats haven't had a nibble of the wares before you buy.

Remember: check woven material for faults... and always haggle.

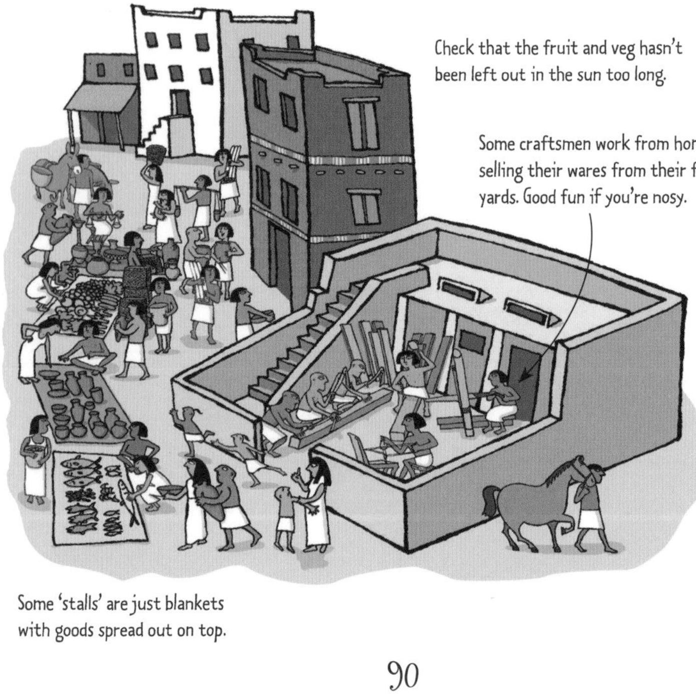

Check that the fruit and veg hasn't been left out in the sun too long.

Some craftsmen work from home, selling their wares from their front yards. Good fun if you're nosy.

Some 'stalls' are just blankets with goods spread out on top.

Buying souvenirs

When you're shopping for trinkets, you should be able to barter (see page 9). It's a good idea to buy yourself a lot of something small and cheap such as beads to barter with at the start of your shopping trip. Oh, and you might want to buy a basket or a bag to carry your purchases in.

Every Egyptian town has at least one market where you'll be able to find all kinds of cheap(ish) souvenirs, from magical gifts such as *shabtis* (see page 76) to more practical items such as papyrus-reed slippers or kitchen pots.

Smell buster

Incense made from fragrant oils and other nice-smelling things are a must-buy when staying in an Egyptian town.

You'll need it to mask the less than fragrant smells you get in a place without plumbing.

It comes in little crystal-like lumps, which you then burn in a special incense burner. You can spot these on market stalls, as they're shaped like an arm, with a hand on the end.

Fabulous faïence

Most markets will have a glazed pottery stall, selling everything from vases to wall tiles. Look for items made from faïence, a heated quartz powder that comes in yellow, white, green, red and a very striking blue.

For top quality crafts, you could buy directly from a workshop of a temple, or even one where the pharaoh's master craftsmen work. It's not legal... but who cares about that when the bribe's big enough?

Feeling scared? Faïence hedgehogs are thought to bring magical powers of protection.

Potty potters

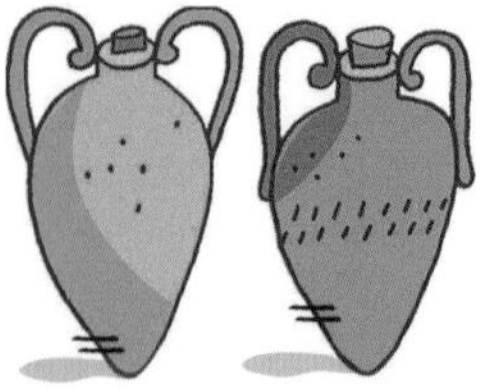

You won't find water bottles on sale in Ancient Egypt, but you can buy pots like these to carry water.

When you're on a long journey in Ancient Egypt and you suddenly feel thirsty, you can't just pop into a café and buy a cold drink. You'll need to take your own water if you want to avoid dehydration.

This means there's one essential purchase when you arrive: a pot with a stopper, to store water. It shouldn't be hard to track down a clay one at a market.

But you could even have a go at making your own. A potter will be more than happy to lend a foreigner his wheel in return for a few beads. (I've added some step-by-step tips on the left so you can avoid a) being laughed at by the potter and b) hitting him with flying clay. Even if he is laughing.)

Making pottery

Step 1 Make sure your lump of clay is in the middle of the wheel.

Step 2 Start spinning.

Step 3 Press your thumb into the middle of the clay to make a hole. Then widen it until you can get your whole hand in.

Step 4 Grip the side of your pot and slowly stretch upwards to make it taller.

Step 5 Press in gently at the top to form the neck.

Step 6 Harden in oven.

Step 7 Look smug.

This potter is making fancy pots and trinkets. You should probably stick to the basics if it's your first time.

You can buy items made with gold and gems without breaking the bank.

Shiny pretty things

If you want to buy an incredibly posh present for a relative (or for yourself) gold is surprisingly good value in Ancient Egypt. It's cheaper than silver, and an awful lot cheaper than it is in the 21st century.

But if you leave your souvenir shopping until the end of your trip, when you're almost out of pepper and copper weights, don't despair. If you want to buy something pretty on a budget, try an amulet strung with a few faïence beads to wear. That way, you get a necklace and magical protection in one.

Top tips for tourists

№ 22: Don't be duped!

Examine expensive 'ebony' items very carefully. Genuine ebony is a heavy black wood. But some traders try to palm you off with cheaper wood coated in black varnish. Try scraping some of the black off as a test.

Smelly goods

Egypt is famous for its perfumes, and you should also be able to find some very elaborately crafted containers to take some home in. (The fish container on the right is a good example.)

Oh, and if you bring back a perfume such as sandalwood, you could sell it at a tidy profit when you get home, as it's very, very expensive in the 21st century.

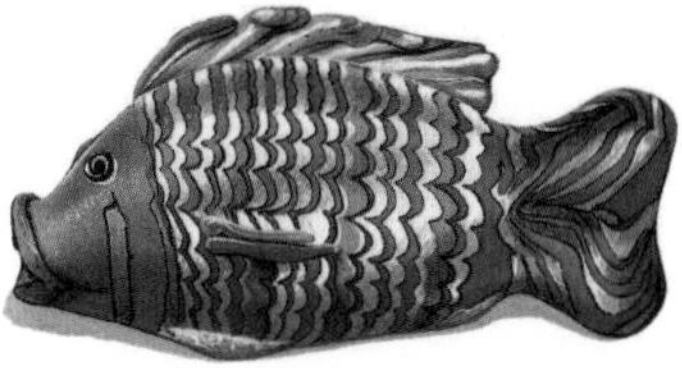

This perfume-holding fish is made from threads of glass.

How to crash a party

Top tips
for tourists

№ 23: Story time

Professional storytellers are in great demand at parties. Egyptian stories are meant to be told rather than read – after all, hardly anyone can read. Really good storytellers can draw audiences from miles around.

Rich Egyptians really know how to have a good time, and they're always throwing lavish parties. No expense will be spared. You can expect to enjoy a seemingly endless stream of food, drink and entertainment, from musicians and dancing girls to jugglers, storytellers and even performing dwarves.

To crash one, listen out for music drifting through an open window, then turn up at the door and shower the host with gifts. Perhaps a little gold you picked up in Nubia, or some ostrich feather fans. Make sure you shower first, though. No amount of presents will make up for whiffy feet. With any luck, you'll be ushered inside with warm smiles.

This is the sort of scene you can expect at a nobleman's party.

Dancing girls performing a well-rehearsed routine
"Shemu keeps looking at you, Hebony. His dad's rich, too."

Fat hat

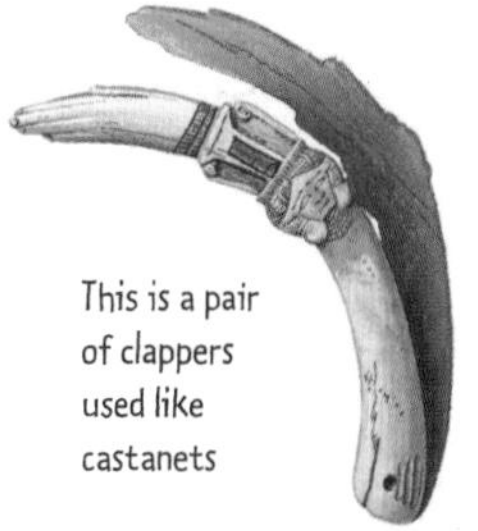

This is a pair of clappers used like castanets

When you arrive, a servant will probably plonk a cone made from fat on your head. But don't get cross - it's special, perfumed fat that's designed to keep you smelling nice and feeling cool during the party.

Take note: men and women sit on opposite sides of the room. It's not because they're shy; it's just how rich Egyptians behave. You should stick to the rules if you want to fit in. You don't want people to think you're a barbarian (even though you are, technically).

One thing to remember is that posh people here don't dance at parties. That's left to the professionals. (If you feel the need for a boogie, head to one of the rowdy inns.)

> *"I have heard that you have abandoned writing and that you whirl around in pleasures..."*
>
> Teacher to a partying pupil

The hosts are sitting on chairs, but most guests sit on stools or cushions.

You'll be eating with your fingers, so servants bring water to wash your hands.

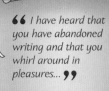

Board games

The most popular board game in Egypt is *Senet*. Stand and watch a game and you might eventually be invited to play.

Senet's played on a chequered board. Each player has seven pieces that they have to move across it, throwing marked sticks to tell them how far they can move. It's a lot like chess or checkers, really.

The best *Senet* boards can be glazed in *faïence*, like this one.

How do Egyptians have fun?

On a hot day (which, let's face it, is most of them) there's nothing Egyptians like more than a swim in the cool Nile. Don't be shy - dive in yourself. It's a great way to make friends, because on a hot day there are always lots of people splashing about in the water. There are lots of games you could join in on, too, plus all kinds of beautiful carved toys and brightly painted balls.

There are loads of toys for children to play with.

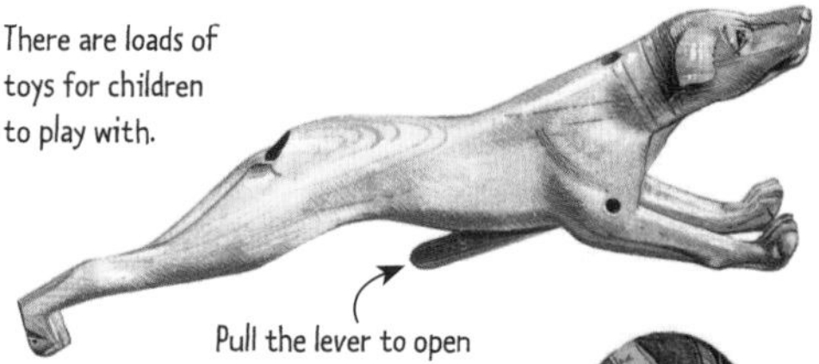

Pull the lever to open the dog's mouth.

These leather balls can be used in all sorts of games.

Hounds and Jackals is another popular game. It's a bit like snakes and ladders.

But playtime is definitely not just for kids. Board games such as *Senet* (see above left) and 'Hounds and Jackals' (which unfortunately I never got to play, so you'll have to find out for yourself) are especially popular with all ages.

All sorts of sports

If you feel as though you need some exercise after all that sitting around on boats, there are all kinds of sports to try, from wrestling, javelin throwing and archery to rowing, hunting and fishing.

If you'd rather just watch, there are lots of local competitions, including organized fights with wooden swords. Just ask around in the taverns or at parties.

Top tips for tourists

№ 24: A quick dip

If you're swimming in the Nile, don't venture into the reed beds. That's where you'll find the most crocodiles. Or rather, they'll find you.

Water games

Down by the river, you'll see men playing 'water jousting'. Only join in if you're a strong swimmer. The aim is to push the other team out of their boat using a pole.

If it's too hot for much activity, you could just go and have a picnic or perhaps take a leisurely boat ride.

Sailing on the Nile is relaxing, as long as you dodge the hippos and crocs.

Egyptians love cats.

Geese are surprisingly popular pets, too.

Pharaoh's pets

Ramesses has a pet lion, called 'Tearer to pieces of his enemies'.

Well, he couldn't really call it Kitty, given that it roars into action alongside his chariot in battle.

He also has a soft spot for two horses that saved his life in battle. Ramesses expects a lot from his pets, doesn't he?

Do Egyptians keep pets?

Absolutely. Egyptians enjoy keeping pet animals as much as they enjoy hunting wild ones. You're likely to see all kinds of creatures in the streets of Ancient Egyptian cities, from cats and dogs to geese and even monkeys. (These can be real pests.)

Then there are the sacred animals, looked after by priests and their servants.

Mind you, they're not exactly pets, given that they each have a god inside them. You wouldn't really talk about having a pet god, would you? Or, at least, you certainly *shouldn't* while you're in Ancient Egypt. Although sacred animals aren't literally gods, it's a good idea to treat them with respect.

Watch your stuff if you spot any pet monkeys in the street – they're fond of a five finger discount.

The sport of kings

In Egypt, hunting is a sport for the rich. But if you've brought enough pepper along with you... that could mean you.

If you'd rather not join in, it's worth watching a hunt, especially if the pharaoh's in town - Ramesses's hunts are grand performances. (The animal death is real, though, so you might want to steer clear if you're an animal lover.)

Hunts usually begin early, so you can't sleep in. The hunters gather and pray (if you're hunting with them, just mumble along) not far from the animals they're after. Gazelles are a popular target.

The hunters charge forward in their chariots, with hunting dogs zipping alongside. Then they fire arrows at their prey (which is probably running like the wind by now), until they bring it down.

Cruel to animals?

Egyptians actually have a very close relationship with the animals they share the Nile with.

Anyone who lives for a long time beside the Nile comes to know the habits of animals, from where they sleep to what they eat.

While the Ancient Egyptians aren't exactly kind to animals all of the time, they respect them – after all, the gods take animal forms sometimes.

If you catch the end of one of the king's hunting trips, you might see a scene like this.

Sometimes the hunting party drives the animals towards a trap, like this bull cornered in a pen. Cheating? Well, can't have the pharaoh taking big risks.

Hippo hunting

Hunting hippos is a way for young men to test their mettle. But I'd advise tourists to steer clear; it's very risky. Hippos can easily flip a boat and trample its crew underwater.

The evil god Set is often shown in hippo form and although hippos sometimes look calm enough, they are not to be messed with.

Feel like some fishing?

If you want to go fishing in Ancient Egypt, don't expect to sit with a rod by the banks of the river, having a picnic and a snooze. A fishing trip usually means standing on a boat, armed with a spear to jab into the fish - no hooks and lines for Egyptian sportsmen.

I suggest you hire a servant for the day. It shouldn't be too expensive, and it saves you having to scan the waters for hippos and crocs while you're trying to spear a fish. Plus, if you hire someone who's a trained fisherman, you can ask his advice about the best craftsmen to buy spears from.

If you want to catch a lot of fish, you could buy a net from a market, but the trouble with that method is that hungry crocodiles find nets full of juicy, shimmering fish very attractive indeed. While spearing fish is tricky, it's less likely to attract vicious animals to share your haul.

These two hunters have bitten off more than they can chew. Hunting a hippo takes a team of men.

A fowl sport

Fowling (catching birds) is seen as a fun way to relax by many rich Egyptians. It's quite a simple sport - you just lob boomerang-like sticks at some birds.

But throwing sticks at birds doesn't seem very sporting to me. It's the sort of thing a boy I knew at school used to do, and he got detention for it, not a sporting prize. (He also used to do that thing where you focus light through a magnifying glass to burn ants. All in all, he was horrible.)

You might see some poorer people by the river catching birds in nets, too. Peasants often do fowling as a job, or so they can eat the birds.

> *"[It's] a happy day when we go down to the marsh... [to] ...snare birds and catch many fishes in the... waters."*
>
> Taken from *The Pleasures of Fishing and Fowling*, an early manuscript

Usually, only poor fisherman use nets to fish with.
"Steady..... steady...."
Hunters use reed boats like these.

Keep it fresh

Many Egyptians keep gardens and if you're staying in a villa, you can enjoy seasonal fruit and veg all year round.

Flood season, around September, means leeks, cucumbers, figs, pomegranates and dates. In spring, expect garlic and peas. Summer is onion season.

Top of the crops

In your travels up and down the Nile, you'll see fields on either side, growing everything from food crops to the flax that's used to make linen thread.

If you're there during flood season, get ready to witness a miracle. The flood leaves behind a layer of rich, black soil, which turns this rainless land into a farmer's paradise, and green shoots poke up along the banks.

The biggest crops are wheat - since Egyptians are such big bread fans, that's not surprising - and a plant called barley, used to bake the bread that's then made into beer.

An eternal supply of wine

Rich Egyptians love their wine. It's called *irp* - yes, I realize what that sounds like, but I'd avoid laughing whenever someone says it if I were you. *Irp* (stop it) is made by brewing grape juice. You might see pictures of this process in tombs - these are supposed to be magical, ensuring the deceased doesn't go thristy.

Grape juice for wine is pressed by hand. Or rather, by foot. Workers grip onto ropes to balance while treading grapes.

The grape juice flows out of the wine press and is collected in a vat.

What farmers get up to

The farmers you'll see have a lot of work to do, but thanks to the fertile soil the Nile leaves behind, it's not as hard as it might be.

The soil just needs a little turning over, or tilling, using simple, light wooden tools with bronze tips. You might also spot animals following the farmers. They're busy treading the seeds that have just been planted into the earth.

In Egypt, cows and other animals do their bit in the fields by trampling seeds into the ground.

Watering the land

Centuries ago, the canny Egyptians built a network of canals to store floodwater. You'll see these canals snaking off from the Nile. They carry the river's water to the fields along a series of connecting channels and ditches.

Actually getting the water onto the fields takes some muscle, though. But a recent invention, the *shadoof* (below), makes life a little easier.

❝ Let us for our master toil. fair is the day and the air is cool. The oxen pull away. the sky our will obeys — let us for our master toil! ❞

A sowers' work song (written by their boss by the sound of it)

A *shadoof* is a bucket fixed to a beam, which is used as a lever to lift the bucket. Take a walk in a field and see if you can spot one.

This is a *shadoof*.

bucket

Lever – this pivots around so the water can be lifted and tipped onto the crops.

Top tips for tourists

Nº 25: Smelly money

Egyptians adore onions, and their potent relative, garlic. So, as well as pepper, you could bring some cloves of garlic to barter with.

Mummies are given strings of onions to symbolize a new set of teeth for the afterlife. So you could bribe your way into the embalmers with a string of onions.

Types of taxes

You (probably) won't have to pay taxes, but just so you know, these are the main ones locals have to pay:

- *Corvée* (work tax)
- Land tax (paid by farmers in grain)
- Craft tax (paid by craftsmen, using goods)
- Hunting and fishing tax (paid in fish and game)

A taxing time

If you stay too long in Ancient Egypt, especially in one place, watch out... you may be forced to work as a slave for a while. Well, sort of like a slave - foreigners who settle in Egypt have to do their *corvée* (see page 43) just like everyone else.

Now, with luck, you should avoid this even if you do stick around, as it's not something people do every year. But if you do have to serve your time, you might find yourself doing some unpleasant or dangerous jobs, such as fighting in the army or working in a mine. Don't think you can dodge it; people who try end up in prison. But unless you stay for years and get a steady job, you shouldn't have to pay other taxes.

By the way, most Egyptian taxes are paid 'in kind' - e.g. a farmer pays in crops.

A taxman and surveyor measure the crops while a resigned farmer and his wife look on.

A working holiday

If you end up running out of pepper and copper weights before the end of your trip, don't despair. If you're there around harvest time, farmers are always looking for an extra pair of hands to help out.

If you get there a little before the harvest, you can enjoy the harvest festival of Min, god of fertility. Note: that's in March *before* harvesting starts.

If you're working in the fields, you might be lucky enough to get a bronze sickle to work with – the latest in farming technology.

Donkeys are often used to carry grain.

Jobs for the girls

If you're a female time tourist, you're definitely better off in Egypt than many other ancient countries. While men and women are far, far from equal in Ancient Egyptian society, women tend to have more rights and opportunities here than they do elsewhere in the ancient world.

For example, although most girls marry and have children young, some women have a career too. They can run businesses or farms (and, yes, pay taxes), or even become a professional dancer. If you want something simpler, you could help out on a farm.

Winnowing (getting rid of the useless bits of grain) is a farming task carried out by women.

Creation tales

One story says that Re, the Creator, emerged from a lotus flower.

Some say Re hatched out of a goose's egg.

Others claim Re was at first a beetle, pushing the Sun, as some beetles roll dung balls.

Household gods must always be kept spick and span.

Everyday gods

My mother always told me not to talk about controversial topics like religion when meeting new people. But in Ancient Egypt, that's tricky advice to follow.

If you're having a chat with an Egyptian, even a discussion about the weather is bound to involve some sky god or other. Spiritual things and everyday life are all mixed up together, and they don't even have a word for religion.

What do people believe?

Egyptian beliefs can seem contradictory. Even when they can agree on who created the universe, their stories about how it happened vary (see left).

As new beliefs arise, they're tagged on to all the old ones. So, if you get the name of a god wrong, don't worry. People will probably just think it's the latest idea.

One unchanging belief to bear in mind when you're trying to understand how Egyptians think is in the balance of *Ma'at* (truth and order) against chaos. *Ma'at* is maintained by temple rituals, people living decently, and the king ruling justly.

Temples and priests

Common folk rarely visit big temples. Instead they pray and leave offerings at small local shrines. Look out for these little statues in the street. They'll be surrounded by food and other gifts. Whatever you do, don't be tempted to have a nibble. You'll find yourself in deep, even painful, trouble.

A lot of the necklaces you'll see people wearing are actually charms to ward off evil spirits. In Egypt, magic isn't seen as different from religion: it's a god-given weapon against the forces of chaos. You never know, it might be worth buying a few charms just in case they're right.

"The Egyptians are religious to excess – beyond any other nation."

Herodotus, Greek historian

If you see a priest carrying food fit for a feast, he's probably going to give it as a sacred offering.

Pure in body...

The most important thing to remember about Egyptian religion as a tourist is that cleanliness isn't next to godliness - it *is* godliness. So if you don't wash, it's not just insulting, it's actually EVIL, as demons are said to live in dirt.

You don't need to take it as far as priests, though. To purify themselves, they wash seven times a day and chew salt, and shave every inch of their bodies when on duty.

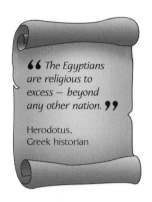

Near a temple, don't be surprised if someone wafts incense up your kilt. He's just smoking out demons.

Isis

Set

Horus

Hathor

Bes

The god squad

Here's a quick guide to some of Egypt's most important gods and goddesses.

Osiris: god of the dead. After being killed by his brother Set, his wife Isis raised him back to life (picture on page 37).

Isis: wife of Osiris, a mistress of magic and a strong woman who tends to get her way.

Set: Osiris's evil brother, god of chaos, the desert, storms and foreigners (nasty beasts!) He's also the god of Ramesses's family, so he's not all bad.

Horus: a sky god, son of Isis and Osiris, who wrestled his dead father's throne from his uncle Set. Pharaohs are seen as an earthly form of Horus, and just like him, many of them fight their relatives to win the throne.

Hathor: Horus's wife. This goddess of love, beauty, music and dance is a real party girl. She takes many forms but is usually a cow. (Beauty really is in the eye of the beholder.)

Bes: the gods' jester, this lovable, pug-ugly pygmy is a popular household god who protects children and families from demons.

Taweret

Taweret: a pregnant hippo with a crocodile's tail, this motherly monster is an ancient goddess of childbirth.

Ma'at

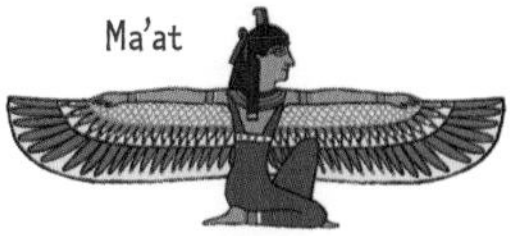

Ma'at: goddess of truth, justice, and the balance of the universe. Her symbol is an ostrich feather, which she wears in her hair.

Anubis

Anubis: jackal-headed god of mummy-making and guardian of graveyards. In the afterlife, he helps to oversee the judgement of the dead, then leads righteous souls to paradise (and the rest to a stickier end).

Thoth

Thoth: long-beaked god of the moon and wisdom, patron of scribes, mathematicians and officials. This wise old bird wrote 42 volumes containing the secrets of the world. You can see his main temple in Hermopolis.

Ptah

Ptah: the ancient creator god of Memphis, patron of craftsmen, and an Underworld deity. Ramesses II made his cleverest son the high priest of Ptah - a political move against the puffed-up priests of Amun-Re.

Sekhmet

Sekhmet: Ptah's wife, this mighty, lion-headed goddess avenges wrongs done to the Sun god Re. As fierce and feared as the midday Sun, her breath can both cause and cure disease. Her priests work as doctors.

When can I go to a festival?

If you hear the sound of trumpets, there will probably be a parade nearby. Follow the noise!

If you stay long enough (but not so long that you have to start paying taxes), you should be able to catch most Egyptian festivals. At these, you might get to see the gods themselves (in statue form, as they're carried out from the temples), accompanied by a frenzy of dancing, feasting and music.

So you can be in the right place at the right time, here's a few tips about when and where to catch the really big ones.

Gods are sometimes taken out of their golden shrines on special occasions.

Opet: the year's most important festival. It takes place in August (the exact date varies), when the statue of Amun-Re is carried through the streets from Karnak to Luxor. When the statue reaches Luxor, the pharaoh himself escorts it into the temple.

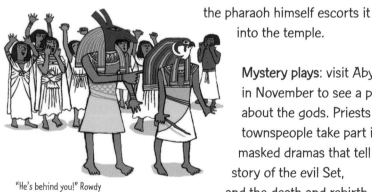

"He's behind you!" Rowdy crowds are all part of the mystery play experience.

Mystery plays: visit Abydos in November to see a play about the gods. Priests and townspeople take part in masked dramas that tell the story of the evil Set, and the death and rebirth of the hero, Osiris.

The Nile will be ablaze with candles and torches as Amun-Re makes his way across the river.

Beautiful Feast of the Valley: this is one of the highlights of the year. It takes place near Thebes at the beginning of summer. Don't miss this one, it's a real treat.

It all kicks off in the early morning, as crowds gather on the cliffs of the West Bank of Thebes. You might need a warm shawl at that time in the morning. The desert can be pretty chilly before sunrise.

Look across the river to the temple of Karnak, and listen out for the songs drifting over the water. Someone will shout: "There he is! There's Amun!" and you'll see the golden statue of Amun-Re lit by floating torches. It's being taken from his temple and ferried to the West Bank tombs.

Acrobats and musicians perform by the river's edge to entertain the crowds, and when the procession reaches the Necropolis, feasts are shared with the spirits of the dead. (The dead just eat the 'spirit' of the food, so there'll be plenty of the solid stuff left over for the living.)

These days Ramesses gets one of his sons to run the Heb-sed (see below).

Heb-sed

Heb-sed is a rare festival, taking place on the 30th anniversary of a pharaoh's reign, and periodically after that. So catching it might require research and a bit of time travel.

In the festival, the ageing king proves his strength by sprinting between two markers.

Egyptian education

Now, you're in Egypt to have fun, not go to school, but knowing a little about Ancient Egyptian education will really help you fit in and avoid embarassing mistakes. For example, if you meet a woman, don't ask where she went to school. Girls don't go to school at all, although rich girls do have lessons at home.

This queen can probably read and write every bit as well as her husband – girls from rich families are taught at home.

What are schools like?

If you want to take a peek inside a school yourself, you'll find schools in all large towns, attached to temples and palaces. But they're not for everyone. Girls don't go, as I said, and only the sons of scribes or people further up the social ladder go to these official schools.

A few villages have schools run by priests or scribes, but these are pricey. Still, reading and writing are rare and very marketable skills in Egypt. So, for anyone who wants to give their children the opportunity to better themselves, it's worth saving up for school fees. (Note: if you can learn some Egyptian writing before you go (see page 115-118) you'll astound the people you meet.)

Scribes

Boys who go to school often end up as scribes, who spend their time copying texts and keeping records.

Most Egyptians can't read or write, so scribes are always in high demand. For some, it's the first step up the ladder of government service.

What do they learn?

Younger children spend all their time learning to read and write, repeating the same thing over and over and over.

Things get a lot less monotonous in secondary school (which starts at about the age of nine or ten), with lessons in history, astronomy, geography, languages, literature and religion, engineering, maths, surveying and accounting. (Though not usually all on the same day.)

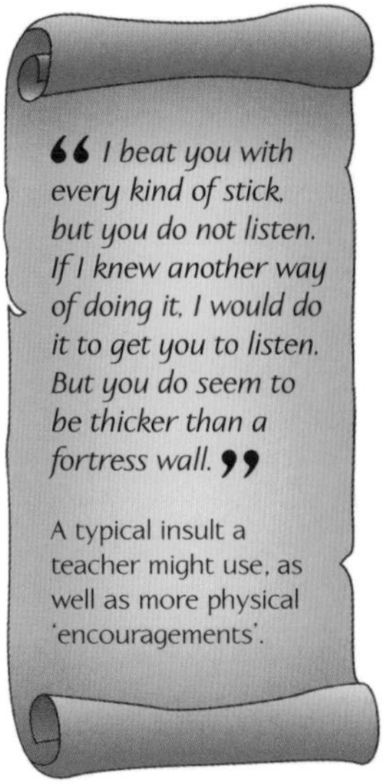
“I beat you with every kind of stick, but you do not listen. If I knew another way of doing it, I would do it to get you to listen. But you do seem to be thicker than a fortress wall.”
A typical insult a teacher might use, as well as more physical 'encouragements'.

School of hard knocks

If you visit a school and you see one of the children being beaten, don't call the *Medjay*. It's normal. Many teachers believe that "a boy's ears are in his back" - in other words, the more you beat a kid, the more he'll listen.

The teachers are often scribes. Some of them are incredibly boring. The boy on the left looks like he's having a sneaky nap.

Speaking the language

You should be able to learn quite a bit of Ancient Egyptian on your trip. Once you're in a country where no one speaks your language - at a time when your language hasn't even been invented yet - it's amazing how quickly you pick things up, especially when you're under pressure.

Nothing makes the word for 'crocodile' stick in your head as well as someone pointing at a crocodile running towards you and screaming the word, "*Mesah! Mesah!*" over and over again in a terrified voice.

A bit of travel vocab

I'm no language expert, so my advice is to hire a scribe for your long boat trips to teach you Egyptian. But here are a few words (spelled in the English alphabet) to help you get where you need to go:

Hy n k (hi-en kay) = Hello

Hy n k neb = Hello lord (say it to anyone who looks important)

Tiu (Tee-oo) = Yes

Nen (as it looks) = No

Hapi (happy) = the Nile (very important!)

Everyday Egyptian

I'm going to tell you about picture writing, a.k.a. hieroglyphics, in a second, but these aren't actually used for everyday stuff. If a scribe was writing a letter or writing some notes, he'd probably use writing that looks like this:

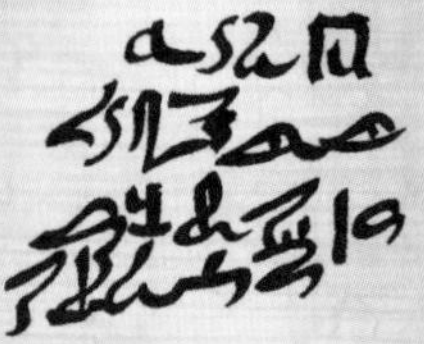

This is a type of handwriting called 'Hieratic'.

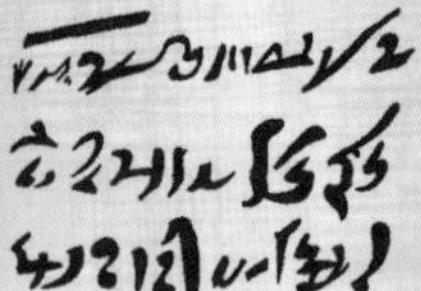

But this type of handwriting is even more widely used. This sort of handwriting is known as 'Demotic'.

Kemit (kemm-it) = Egypt (though literally, it means 'the black land')

Deshret (desh-ret) = the desert (literally, 'the red land')

Shemu (shem-oo) = Upper Egypt

Ta-menu (tar men-oo) = Lower Egypt

Depet (depp-ett) = Ship

djai (jai) = to ferry across

khadi (cardy) = go downstream (North)

khenti (kenty) = to sail upstream (South)

Words in pictures

As I said earlier, the Egyptians use symbols that we call hieroglyphs, a type of picture writing. Egyptians call them *medu netjer*, 'the words of god'.

This is because the god Thoth is supposed to have invented them. You'll see these symbols all over the place, from temple walls to carved *shabtis* on sale in the market.

Think of them as an incredibly complex secret code. I have to confess the notes I made about hieroglyphics are a real mess, so I've only managed to piece together a few tips on decoding them. But they should give you somewhere to start, at least.

Top tips for tourists

№ 26: Greeting the King

If you meet the pharaoh, be very careful how you talk to him. Don't use his name – say '*hem ef*' or 'your majesty'.

If you're talking to someone else, call him '*Nisu bety*' or 'King of Upper and Lower Egypt', as well as 'Ramesses' and '*Sa Re*', or son of Re. The more names the better.

Thoth, the ibis-headed god of wisdom, and guardian of scribes, is said to have invented writing. (He's clearly no bird-brain.)

Finding hieroglyphs

You're most likely to see hieroglyphs carved in stone, in or outside temples and tombs, or other official buildings. You can also buy hieroglyphs written in ink on papyrus.

When you see a set of pictures in a frame, like the one below, it's a pharaoh's name.

Look out for them in temples and tombs.

These hieroglyphs stand for Neb-Kheperu-Re, one of of Tutankhamun's names. The frame or 'cartouche' gives the name magical protection.

More than pictures

I've been talking about hieroglyphics as picture writing, but it's not just a question of drawing a picture of what you're talking about. After all, you'd have trouble writing anything that wasn't about physical objects. (For example, in the sentence, "I hate Mondays", what could you draw? What does a 'Monday' look like?)

Sound signs

Some signs look like the object they stand for, but many of the 700 or so hieroglyphs stand for sounds. But how can you tell what kind you're looking at? Simple. A sign with a stroke under it means what it looks like. No stroke? It stands for a sound. (Sadly, scribes sometimes forget to add the stroke.)

A cobra-shaped sign with a stroke under it just means 'cobra'.

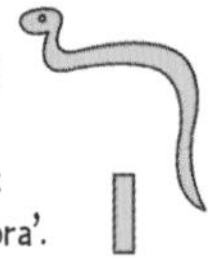

A cobra sign on its own stands for the sound 'dj'.

Sound signs are joined together to make up hieroglyphic words. In English, for example, it would be like using images of a bee and leaf to stand for the word 'belief'.

Vowel trouble

Egyptians don't usually write down the vowel sounds in a word, even though they say them. So, the word for 'beautiful' is said *nefer*, but the signs read *nfr*. Also, scribes tend to put the signs in whatever order looks pretty, so things can get confusing.

WJ TGMN
HM TP SHRJ
NT BJK!!
Reading and writing hieroglyphs is HARD. Anyone who can do it well's my hero!

Reading order

Even the order you read hieroglyphs in works like some kind of spy code. They can be written from right to left or left to right. If the people and animals face right, start from the right, and the other way around.

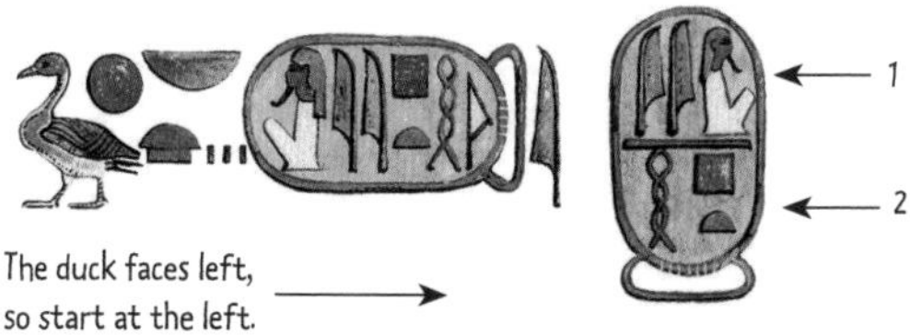

The duck faces left, so start at the left.

Common hieroglyphs

These hieroglyphs stand for particular sounds

Some tricky Egyptian sounds such as the hieroglyph that looks like an arm ('ar' as in far) are simplified. It's really more like a gargle. (Practise it in private.)

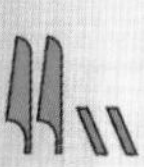
'y' as in **y**es

'j' as in **j**ump

'b' as in **b**oot

'm' as in **m**oon

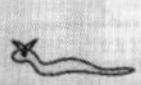
'f' as in **f**rog

hard 'g' as in **g**ood

'h' as in **h**ouse

'n' as in **n**avy

'ch', a bit like 'h' in **h**uge

'i' or 'a' as in mach**i**ne or f**a**r

Looking up royalty

If you see hieroglyphs with a frame around them, like this, they'll stand for a pharaoh's name. Here's how to read this one:

When a god's name forms part of another name it's written first out of respect, even if, as here, it isn't the first part of the spoken name.

The cartouche tells us that this is a royal name.

The bird faces right, so we read from right to left.

These symbols make up an extra title, meaning 'Ruler of Thebes'.

Cartouche key

1. twt, said 'tut': the Ancient Egyptian word for 'image'.
2. This symbol stands for 'ankh', meaning 'living'.
3. Said as 'Amun', the god of Thebes.

So the pharaoh is... Tutankhamun! That means 'living image of Amun'. The reason the last sound in the name is put first is because Amun is a god. It's to show respect. (Even if it makes the thing almost impossible to read... grumble.)

A tricky business

If you can't make sense of any of the hieroglyphs you see on your travels, don't feel too bad about it.

People stopped using these symbols in Egypt around the 4th Century and their meanings were completely forgotten over time. It actually took until the 19th Century for anyone to puzzle out what they meant again. So you're not alone.

This sign on its own means 'son'. You can see why it took a long time to work out what hieroglyphs meant.

Well, I think that almost wraps it up. But before I finish, I have a few last little titbits for you.

In the final pages of this book, you'll find a timeline showing the reigns of various pharaohs, and some other important bits of Ancient Egyptian history.

There's also a guide to the various pharaohs, as I'm sure they'll come up at some point in conversation while you're in Egypt. Oh, and I've noted down a few definitions of Egyptian people, things, ideas and habits that I mentioned earlier, so you can remind yourself what they mean.

So, let me just say, "Ankh wedja seneb." ("May you live long, prosper and be healthy.") And good luck!

M xxx

Timeline of Ancient Egypt

This timeline shows the most important pharaohs of Egypt. It's divided up into 'kingdoms' and 'dynasties', but you don't need to worry too much about those. They're probably more useful to historians than tourists.

Early Dynastic Period

c. 3100–2686 BC

Dynasty 1
c. 3100 BC King **Menes** unites Upper and Lower Egypt and builds a capital at Memphis. Kings are buried in mud-brick tombs at the town of Abydos.

Dynasty 2
A number of poorly-known kings, buried at Abydos and Sakkara.

Old Kingdom

c. 2686–2181 BC

Dynasty 3 *c.* 2686–2613 BC
Imhotep builds King **Djoser**'s step pyramid at Sakkara.

Dynasty 4 *c.* 2613–2494 BC
c. 2613–2589 BC King **Sneferu** builds straight-sided pyramid.
c. 2589–2566 BC Reign of **Khufu.** Great Pyramid built at Giza.
c. 2558–2532 BC **Khafre** (Chephren)
c. 2532–2504 BC **Menkaure** (Mycerinus)

Dynasty 5 *c.* 2494–2345 BC
c. 2375–2345 BC King **Unas**'s tomb has the first carved Pyramid Texts.

Dynasty 6 *c.* 2345–2181 BC
c. 2278–2184 BC **Pepi II** rules for 94 years.

3rd Intermediate Period

c. 1069–664 BC

Dynasty 21 *c.* 1069–945 BC Egypt is split between northern rulers and priests of Amun-Re in Thebes.

Dynasty 22 *c.* 945–715 BC Reign of Libyan kings from Bubastis, city of the cat goddess Bast

Dynasty 23 *c.* 818–715 BC A family of Libyan kings ruling from Herakleopolis, Hermopolis and Thebes

Dynasty 24 *c.* 727–715 BC A line of two pharaohs who rule from the city of Sais in the Delta

Dynasty 25 *c.* 747–656 BC Rulers from Nubia take control of Egypt and establish a huge African kingdom. Their reign is finally ended by invading forces from Assyria.

End of 25th dynasty overlaps with start of 26th

Late Period

c. 664–332 BC

Dynasty 26 664–525 BC This dynasty united Egypt again.

Dynasty 27 525–404 BC Conquest by Persia. One Persian king loses his entire army in the desert.

Dynasties 28–30 404–343 BC Egyptian princes overthrow the Persians and rule Egypt.
Nectanebo I 380–362 BC restores many temples.
Nectanebo II 360–343 BC last native Egyptian king

343–332 BC A second conquest by Persian kings.

332 BC **Alexander the Great** of Macedon (northern Greece) conquers Egypt. His heirs form a dynasty, the Ptolemies. The last Ptolemy is the famous **Cleopatra**. After her death in 30 BC, the Romans rule Egypt.

Note: During the Intermediate Periods the rule of Egypt was divided again, so dynasties often overlap.

1st Intermediate Period
c. 2181–2055 BC

Dynasties 7 and **8** c. 2181–2125 BC
These dynasties featured many kings who only had short reigns.

Dynasties 9 and **10**
c. 2160–2025 BC
A new line of kings rules from the city of Herakleopolis. Down south, in Upper Egypt, the Prince of Thebes is in charge.

Middle Kingdom
c. 2055–1650 BC

Dynasty 11 c. 2055–1985 BC
Egypt is re-unified by a Prince of Thebes, **Mentuhotep II**. Thebes becomes the capital.

Dynasty 12 c. 1985–1795 BC
Amenemhet I and his son rebuild Egypt, conquering Nubia and building many forts. A time of great art.

Dynasty 13 c. 1795–1650 BC
The short reigns of about 65 kings.

Dynasty 14 c. 1750–1650 BC Princes who rule at the same time as Dynasty 13. Some of Lower Egypt overrun by a people known as the Hyksos.

2nd Intermediate Period c. 1650–1550 BC

Dynasty 15 c. 1650–1550 BC
The reign of the Hyksos kings in the north. Their capital is Avaris, close to site of the later Per Ramesses.

Dynasties 16 and **17**
c. 1650–1550 BC Theban kings who rule at the same time as the 15th dynasty. The last kings of the 17th dynasty, **Tao II** and his son **Kamose**, begin a war to kick out the Hyksos.

New Kingdom
c. 1550–1069 BC

Dynasty18 c. 1550–1295 BC
c. 1550–1525 BC Reign of **Ahmose**, conqueror of the Hyksos
c. 1525–1504 BC **Amenhotep I** enlarges Amun's temple at Karnak.
c. 1479–1457 BC **Hatshepsut**, a queen who rules as a king
c. 1479–1425 BC **Thutmose III**, the greatest warrior pharaoh
c. 1400–1390 BC **Thutmose IV**, who uncovers the Sphinx
c. 1390–1352 BC **Amenhotep III** builds the temple at Luxor
c. 1352–1336 BC **Amenhotep IV (Akhenaten)**, the heretic pharaoh
c. 1336–1327 BC **Tutankhamun**, the 'boy king'
c. 1323–1295 BC **Horemheb**, a former general and wise lawmaker

Dynasty 19 c. 1305–1186 BC
c. 1295–1294 BC The brief reign of **Ramesses I**
c. 1294–1279 BC **Seti I**, a strong ruler, great warrior and builder
c. 1279–1213 BC Reign of **Ramesses II** (This is when you should visit.)
Dynasty 20 c. 1186–1069 BC **Setnakht**, and then more **Ramesses**-es!

Who's who

This 'Who's who' of Ancient Egypt is largely made up of pharaohs, since they're by far the most important people in the country. With over 300 rulers, however, only a few can be listed. Dates of reigns in brackets; the 'c.' sign means 'roughly': even experts aren't sure *exactly* when they lived.

Ahmose (*c.*1550-1525BC): Ahmose came to the throne as a child, though this isn't uncommon among pharaohs. He freed Egypt from the Hyksos, a people from the East who were occupying much of Egypt at the time.

Ahmose Nefertari (Around the same time as Ahmose): Ahmose's sister, who was also his wife. After his death, she ruled in place of their son **Amenhotep I** until he was old enough to rule himself. They founded the tomb workers' village (see page 60), where they were worshipped as gods after their deaths.

Akhenaten (*c.*1352-1336BC): first took the throne as **Amenhotep IV**. This controversial king abolished all gods apart from a sun god, Aten, renamed himself and built a new capital, Akhetaten (modern Amarna). After his death, Egypt went back to having many gods, his capital was abandoned and all of his monuments were destroyed. That'll show him.

Cleopatra VII (51-30BC) Egypt's most famous queen, and its last pharaoh. Cleopatra was one of the Ptolemies, a Macedonian (northern Greek) dynasty that ruled for nearly 300 years. Killed herself with snake poison after getting into serious trouble with some Romans.

Djoser (Some time around 2686-2613 BC): king of Egypt, notable for having the first step pyramid, at Sakkara.

Hatshepsut (*c.*1479-1457BC): a queen who ran things for her young nephew, Thutmose III, but then seized power and reigned sucessfully as 'king' for over 20 years. She even wore a fake beard. Mind you, so did a lot of pharaohs, as they shaved all over.

Horemheb (*c.*1323-1295BC 18th dynasty) a former army general, he spent much of his reign wiping out the memory of Akhenaten. He also reformed the justice system, passing tough new laws to punish corrupt officials.

Imhotep (3rd dynasty): an official in Djoser's reign, he designed the first step pyramid.

Khufu (Cheops) (*c.*2589-2566BC 4th dynasty): son of **Sneferu**, his pyramid, the Great Pyramid, was the biggest ever built. His son **Khafre** and grandson **Menkaure** built the other pyramids at Giza.

Menes (*c.*3100BC): a king of Upper Egypt, he conquered Lower Egypt, uniting the two kingdoms as the first king of the First Dynasty. Who Menes was is lost in the mists of time, but it may be a second name for the early King Narmer ('Catfish') or his son, King Aha ('Fighter').

Mentuhotep II (*c.*2055-2004BC 11th dynasty) Prince of Thebes who became the first pharaoh of the Middle Kingdom.

Nefertari (19th dynasty): chief queen of Ramesses II, and the love of his life. He built one of the temples at Abu Simbel for her. She also has a spectacular tomb in the Valley of the Queens.

Who's who continued

Nefertiti (18th dynasty): queen of Egypt and wife of Akhenaten. Renowned for her good looks, her name means 'beauty has come'. Not to be confused with Nefertari or Ahmose Nefertari.

Pepi II (*c.* 2278-2184BC 6th dynasty): the last king of the Old Kingdom. After taking the throne at the age of six, he reigned for 94 years - the longest reign in history.

Ramesses I (*c.*1295-1294BC 19th dynasty): a former army officer and vizier to Horemheb, who, having no son, let his trusted comrade reign alongside him. When Horemheb died shortly after, Ramesses founded the 19th dynasty. Old himself, Ramesses I crowned his son, Seti, in his own lifetime, to avoid battles for the throne.

Ramesses II (*c.*1279-1213BC 19th dynasty): known as Ramesses the Great, largely due to his extensive building and flair for publicity. Early in his reign he fought the Hittites at the Battle of Kadesh, in Syria. Later, he signed a peace treaty with their king, Hattusili.

Seti I (*c.*1294-1279BC 19th dynasty): A strong leader, Seti I expanded the frontiers of Egypt, and built up many temples. His huge tomb is considered the finest in the Valley of the Kings.

Tutankhamun (*c.*1336-1327BC 18th dynasty): Akhenaten's son, he'll find fame in 1922 when his tomb is found by archaeologist Howard Carter.

Thutmose III (*c.*1479-1425BC 18th dynasty): One of Egypt's greatest warrior kings.

What's what

amulet: a lucky charm

cataract: a shallow stretch of the Nile where boulders make it hard to navigate

delta: a flat, often triangular, region of mud that spreads out at the mouth of a river

Duat: the Underworld, where Egyptians go when they die, ruled over by the god Osiris

dynasty: a series of rulers from the same family

embalming: drying out a body to preserve it after death

faïence: a type of glazed material, often bright blue

hieroglyphics: Egyptian writing, which uses symbols known as hieroglyphs to stand for sounds, things or ideas

Ma'at: truth, justice, the balance of the universe; also seen as a goddess

Medjay: the Egyptian police

mummy: an embalmed body wrapped in bandages

necropolis: a cemetery; the word means 'city of the dead'. For example, the area of the royal tombs in Thebes, on the West Bank of the Nile

obelisk: a tall, square column with a pyramid-shaped top

ostracon (plural **ostraca**): broken pottery or stone used to write on

papyrus: a type of reed; also the name for a sort of paper made from this reed

pharaoh: a king of Egypt

scribe: someone who writes and copies texts and keeps records

shrine: a small temple, or a container for a god's statue

stela (plural **stelae**): a stone carved with inscriptions, which are often prayers

vizier: a pharaoh's chief minister

Index

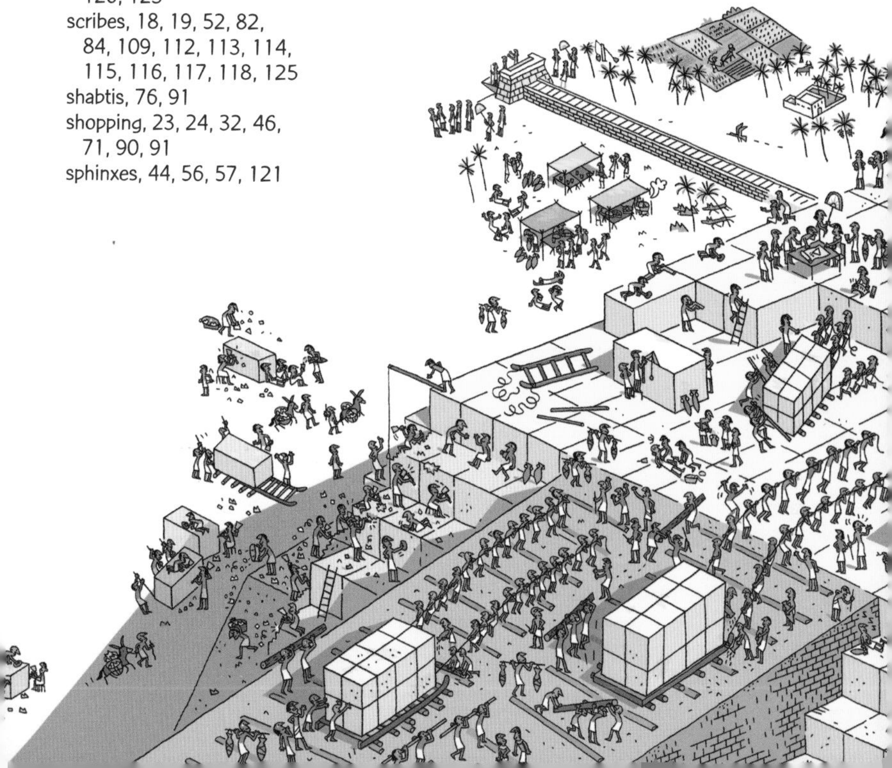

Acknowledgements:

Edited by Jane Chisholm

Digital manipulation by Keith Furnival

History consultant: Dr. Anne Millard

Hieroglyphs based on the Aegyptus typeface, created by George Douros

This edition first published in 2014 by Usborne Publishing Ltd.,
Usborne House, 83-85 Saffron Hill, London EC1N 8RT, England.
www.usborne.com